(BLACK AND WHITE

THE INCONVENIENT

TRUTH

ABOUT

CLIMATE CHANGE

overpopulation and **deforestation**

as the

self-destruction of humankind

© Copyright 2020 George Warehouseman

All Rights Reserved.

Protected with www.protectmywork.com

(Book Formatting by Derek Murphy @Creativindie)

> *I would rather have questions that cannot be answered, than answers that cannot be questioned.*
>
> /Richard Feynman/

President Donald Trump once said that he was going to plant one billion trees. And I applaud that! The reason for my appreciation is the realisation that **Climate Change** has been caused by **Deforestation**. However, Deforestation itself is caused by **Overpopulation**. So, no, **Elon Musk** is **wrong** about this planet having not enough people, and he is wrong about his warnings that we are going to die out. In fact, we should start to **reduce the number of humans** on this planet and **plant back forests** at a panicking speed. That is the only way to **avoid a hard landing**.

My hope is that after reading the facts of this book, many climate activists will switch the focus of their fight against **CO2** emissions to **deforestation** and **overpopulation**.

Don't take my word for it! The arguments and facts exposed in this book are very convincing. Here, I will explain and prove how, according to these facts, our planet can only sustain **less than one billion people** before we start to leave a lasting imprint on our planet's ecosystems. And the main cause of all **climate problems**, starting from **higher temperatures**, **melting of ice caps and glaciers**, and **changing rain patterns**, stems from **Deforestation**. Facts about **Overpopulation** are truly **terrifying**! The essence of all those facts is under the **INTRODUCTION**.

Closer to the end of this book, I will also provide some suggestions for what we have to do to solve all the current problems. And no, those ideas do not include killing off humans. However, if we keep the existing numbers, then it will lead to the killing of the majority of humans by Nature itself. And solving Climate Change problem is much easier than you think too!

Just read it! It's an absolute must!

***

PLEASE, PLEASE, PLEASE…

- If you find the facts in this book worthy of your attention and suitable for sharing with a wider population, please mention the book to others and spread the word!

- Alternatively, you can consider buying some of my other books:

    1. **WHERE DO THE UNIVERSE AND LIFE COME FROM**
    2. **The Mystery of Gravitational Attraction**
    3. **How MAGNETISM, TIDES and GRAVITY Actually Work**
    4. **The True Distances to Stars and Size of the Universe**
    5. **The Inconvenient Truth About Climate Change**

- To help me with further investigation of this and many other topics in science, you can consider supporting me by buying a coffee:

    buymeacoffee.com/jurisbogdanovs

All of these books can be found **on Amazon**! All of them address facts (*within the given scope*) that scientists have ignored or misinterpreted. There are no advances in our understanding of Nature if we allow these things to go unchallenged!

Note! – Some titles might be slightly changed.

Table of Contents

A SHORT DESCRIPTION OF CHAPTERS VI

INTRODUCTION 1

WHAT IS WRONG WITH CLIMATE CHANGE 13

    WHAT IS WRONG WITH THE CLAIM ABOUT THE GREENHOUSE EFFECT! 13

    TYPES AND ESSENCE OF HUMIDITY! 17

    THE FAKE NEWS ABOUT THE ROLE OF CO2 EMISSIONS IN CLIMATE CHANGE........ 23

    TRANSPIRATION AND THE IMPORTANCE OF TREES IN HUMIDITY LEVELS 29

    SCIENTISTS DON'T KNOW HOW CLOUDS ARE FORMED 36

THE LEVELS AND ROLE OF DEFORESTATION 39

    THE ROLE OF CLOUDS IN CLIMATE CHANGE 46

    THE LEVELS OF DEFORESTATION 53

    WE ARE KILLING THE PLANET THROUGH DEFORESTATION! 63

    THE PROBLEM WITH THE GLACIERS, MOUNTAIN TOPS, AND POLAR CAPS. 66

    DEFORESTATION VISUALIZED. 69

    THE WORLD WILL RUN OUT OF DRINKING WATER BECAUSE OF DEFORESTATION.. 72

    THE WORLD WILL RUN OUT OF HABITABLE LAND FOR AGRICULTURE 74

    THE OVERPOPULATION OF THE UNITED KINGDOM 86

    THE OVERPOPULATION OF THE WORLD 96

    MPEMBA EFFECT AND CLIMATE CHANGE... 106

HUMANS SHOULDN'T INTERFERE IN CLIMATE CHANGE APART FROM
RESTORING IT TO THE ORIGINAL STATE 113

    THE MIRACLE THAT SAVED YELLOWSTONE PARK: 114

    THE REINTRODUCTION OF WOLVES 114

    CHINA'S ATTEMPT TO INCREASE CROP YIELDS BY KILLING OFF SPARROWS TURNED SOUR 117

    THE DANGERS OF GEOENGINEERING OR CLIMATE ENGINEERING 118

    NOW, THE MOST IMPORTANT QUESTION - WHAT TO DO TO SAVE THE WORLD? 131

AUTHORS PAGE 151

THIS AND THAT 161

ABOUT OTHER BOOKS OF MINE... 172

A short description of chapters

INTRODUCTION

In this chapter, you will be presented with the core facts of everything contained in this book. For those of you who don't have much time to read, this chapter will provide all the necessary information in the form of bullet points. Essentially, this chapter serves as the essence of the entire book. "If, after this chapter, you read the chapter about why humans shouldn't interfere with the climate using several climate engineering methods, then you will know everything you need to know.

What is Wrong with Climate Change

Climate change is real. However, CO_2 emissions and higher temperatures aren't the only things that have changed since the Industrial Revolution began. Many other factors have also changed, and on a much larger scale than CO_2 emissions.

What is wrong with the claim about the Greenhouse Effect

There are many inconsistencies in the scientific theory of the Greenhouse Effect. For instance, the Greenhouse Effect is impossible in an open atmosphere. In the end, it should be clear that the stories about the Greenhouse Effect in the atmosphere are more akin to pseudoscience.

Types and essence of humidity

For the sake of this book, I will focus on two types of humidity. One is relative humidity, and the other is specific humidity. One describes humidity at any given temperature, while the other describes the total amount of water in the air. These facts lead to seemingly absurd observations – the air has been becoming increasingly drier for many decades, while the total amount of water in the air is increasing. This, finally, helps explain the changing rainfall patterns.

The fake news about the role of CO2 emissions in climate change

You shouldn't be surprised if you have no clear understanding of the amount of CO2 in our atmosphere. You might know the number, but that figure doesn't give you a true sense of the scale of CO2 in the atmosphere. In this chapter, all of that will be explained. A hint – CO2 levels in the air are tiny.

Transpiration and the importance of trees in humidity levels

Here, you will learn about the role of forests in air humidity and cloud formation. It turns out that everything science has already learned about forests clearly confirms that they directly affect humidity, temperatures, rain patterns, and more. The process through which they do this is called 'transpiration. And the amount of fully grown forests on our planet is very important to maintain healthy water cycles.

The levels and role of deforestation

The role of forests in maintaining healthy water cycles is incredibly important. Deforestation leads to shortages of drinking water all around the globe. Here, you will learn how deforestation is not only responsible for rising temperatures, but also for disrupting rain patterns, causing droughts, and leading to floods. To ensure our survival, we must replant all those annihilated forests. Readers should be aware of these facts to make informed decisions.

The role of clouds in climate change

The formation of clouds is not fully understood yet. There are speculations, but so far, everything is indeed theoretical and might be true. However, no one knows for sure, as we lack easy access to them. Yet, it's easy to recognize that the role of clouds in the climate is enormous. You'll learn about all of this in this chapter.

The levels of Deforestation

The scale of deforestation is mind-blowing. Given the role of forests in ecosystems, we should all be very concerned and committed not only to stopping deforestation but also to starting afforestation immediately. However, this topic is largely ignored by mainstream science, politicians, and journalists. This neglect is a consequence of poor education and an inability to gather and analyse facts.

The problem with the glaciers, mountain tops, and polar caps

In this chapter, you will see how changes in relative humidity are most likely the cause of the disappearance of ice caps on the poles, mountain tops, and glaciers.

The world will run out of habitable land for agriculture

Overpopulation leads to deforestation, which in turn leads to droughts, wildfires, and soil erosion during floods. All these factors contribute to the disappearance of arable land, with what remains being much less fertile. We are on the brink of running out of land for agriculture as it is.

The overpopulation of the United Kingdom

"The country that is unable to feed itself due to shortages of arable land still keeps all doors open to immigration. When climate change starts causing trouble with food supply, the UK will find itself in a catastrophe. Not a single scientist, journalist, or politician is blowing the whistle.

Mpemba Effect and climate change...

This effect explains how and why the upper layers of the atmosphere are cooling while the opposite is happening near Earth's surface.

Humans shouldn't interfere in climate change apart from restoring it to the original state

"This is the second most important part of this book, following the Introduction. Here, you will understand why all currently applied methods to mitigate the consequences of climate change, such as cloud seeding, cloud brightening, and CO2 capture, are very bad ideas with potentially tragic consequences. Based on these methods, the conspiracy theory about Chemical Trails was born. And, as usual, it is partly right.

Now, the most important question - WHAT TO DO to save the world?

Clearly, here I will mention some actions we should have started implementing 'yesterday'. I cannot promise that all necessary actions are included in this list, along with their importance. One thing is clear – we don't have time for discussions. We must begin afforesting the world and drastically reduce paper and meat consumption to allow as many trees as possible to thrive. Some of the best places to start afforestation are deserts. There are already many great and successful examples of afforestation in China and Africa. We must start now!

INTRODUCTION

Dear Reader,

With this letter I will try to prove to you (with very solid and officially confirmed facts) that overpopulation on our planet is real, and it is the main cause of the climate crisis. Overpopulation has led to enormous levels of deforestation. Humans have interfered in the cycles of nature to provide the growing number of our species with food. These factors have led to and continue to advance climate change. Also, in this text, I will try to prove to you that we can no longer escape the so-called hard landing caused by human-made climate change. However, we can still save the planet and humanity in general. Unfortunately, and I will explain this here too, the vast majority of people will die because of these predicaments. It will be caused by global food shortages and starvation, which will lead to even bigger migration of nations and even wars, as the food shortages will be all over the world. Believe me, we are on the doorstep of these events unless we act swiftly. The best course of action right now is to start a rapid worldwide afforestation. What I would like from you is your voice in raising these problems in front of the whole world. Remember, if we don't do that, the consequences will be very dire.

Let us start with facts about OVERPOPULATION!

In total, there are **104 sq.km.** of habitable land on this planet. If we divide this land by **8 billion people**, then each person has only **1.3 hectares (3 acres)** of habitable land. This is already an extremely small amount. A standard **FIFA football pitch** is around **0.7 ha** or **(2 acres)** large. So, each person on this planet right now would have slightly **less than 2 standard FIFA football pitches**. Some people think it is a lot. But wait for the other facts... Trust me, we are close to a catastrophe.

According to scientific data, feeding one adult for a year requires between **0.5 to 5 hectares (1.25 to 11.25 acres)** of land. Other scientists estimate this range to be **from 0.2 hectares (half an acre) to 4 hectares (10 acres)**. The amount of land needed heavily depends on our diet, body size, and the fertility and weather conditions of the land. To keep your interest in this topic fresh, you should know that right now **in England** there is **only 0.2 ha (0.5 acres)** of land **per person** left as it is... That's the **size of tennis pitch**. This means that in case of global food shortages, England will face a catastrophe.

Keep in mind that this amount of land does not exclude forests, national parks, areas covered by human settlements, and roads. Settlements and roads in England take up a very large proportion of land... The smallest amount of land needed to feed oneself for a year is for those who live on plant-based diets. Eating poultry also doesn't add much to the required territory. However, if we want to enjoy beef and dairy products, as we do today, then we need the maximum amount of land to feed one person. As you can see, **if all 8 billion people were adults** and wanted a full spectrum of food in their diet, we would need around **320 to 400 sq.km. of arable land already**. As I mentioned at the beginning, our **planet only has 104 sq.km.** of habitable land as it is. So, in this model, we would need at least four times more land than the planet currently has to feed those 8 billion beef and dairy-eating adults.

Note: If the previous facts didn't scare you already, keep reading!

Of course, not all people on this planet are adults, and hundreds of millions of people suffer from insufficient food supplies throughout their lives. This is how we get around the problem of food shortages. But that won't last long. After all, we are poisoning the land with pesticides, fertilizers, and other daily-used chemicals. The more of us there are on this planet, the larger the amount of chemical pollution we create. We are also recklessly depleting the fertility of the existing land with those chemicals. Additionally, there is the problem of diminishing water supplies in far too many regions across the world. This issue is explained very well in the documentary "Pumped Dry", and we will address it too in this very letter. All of this will significantly affect food supplies in the very near future, as all of these problems keep growing, as does the number of humans on this planet.

Despite these facts, journalists, politicians, businessmen (Elon Musk...), and even scientists keep shouting from all rooftops that there are not enough people on this planet, and we will run out of workers if we stop breeding like crazy. Nobody is talking about the fact that with the current density of people on our planet, we have around 77 people per sq. km already on the habitable land of our planet. Clearly, there are already too many people on Earth. In fact, at least 10 times too many... How do I know that this is the case? Keep reading, and you will find out!

Some people, who do not like reality and facts, say that the Netherlands is a good example of how humanity can easily feed not only the existing 8 billion but even twice as many. After all, the Netherlands is the most densely populated country in Europe, with more than 500 people per sq. km. Despite this, it is the third-largest food exporter in the world.

However, the food export of the Netherlands is small compared to the volumes of the USA and China. They also have many natural advantages that allow them to achieve this incredibly high productivity. They have a good climate, flat and very fertile land, and their own gas resources that allow them to heat their greenhouses and use it as an energy source for many other needs. Additionally, they don't have any water shortages.

Clearly, not many countries have such luxury. For instance, most of Russia is considered habitable too. Yet, with its weather conditions and poor soil on most of its territory, the yield will be several times lower than it is in the Netherlands. The same is true for the majority of lands in other countries as well. So, no, the Netherlands is not proof that humanity can achieve the same productivity anywhere. It cannot be used as an example for that at all.

Next are some more facts!

I already told you that each human being on this planet has only 1.3 hectares (3 acres) of habitable land as of now. What I didn't mention is that one-third of this land is still covered by forests, and another quarter of it should be afforested back for reasons soon to be explained in this letter. This leaves each human with only half of this land for food production. Namely, **we each have around 1 football pitch (2 acres) of land**, and it would have the average fertility of all lands on ours planet. Not too good prospects, if you ask me.

So, when the correct number of forests is restored (trust me, we have no choice but to do that!), each of us will be left with slightly less than **0.7 hectares (2 acres)** of land. This is an incredibly small amount of land to survive on, especially with the changing climate that will affect crop yield.

To provide all people with food from such a small territory, we will need to use a lot of chemicals and fertilizers. But that poisons the soil. Poisoning the soil at some point might and will lead to a collapse of fertility altogether. This will lead to crop failures in the long run. With our intensive farming, we are also damaging and changing the other participants of natural cycles, such as insects, birds, and microorganisms that live in the soil, and fish that live in the waters. That cannot go on forever, especially because our numbers and volumes of poisons released into nature keep increasing. I wish these were the only ill effects from human activity imposed on nature... But for some reason, we only keep flogging the CO2 emissions, which are the least of our problems.

The **UK currently provides only 60% of all the food it consumes**, and the number of humans in it keeps growing. The reason for that growth is the open-door policy to immigration. Politicians pretend that they are fighting hard to reduce these numbers, but, in reality, they have created too many legal options for it to increase. Illegal immigration is tiny compared to the legal one. But the country is heavily overpopulated already. As I said, the UK cannot feed itself anymore. When it comes to **England**, it **can only provide some 20% to 30% of the food it consumes**. Yet, have you ever heard a single politician addressing this problem of overpopulation in the face of possible global food shortages caused by climate change? Even worse, I have been trying to reach out to media and politicians of all kinds in the UK about this topic and received back a complete silence. Those organisations include **GB News**, **Talk TV**, **British Parliament**, and others. I have addressed organisations and individuals alike. Not a single person has addressed this problem. And I am not surprised about the likes of **Radio LBC** or **BBC**, who by definition are biased and ignorant, and often even demonstrably wrong. But what is the problem with all the other people? It truly is a mystery, why Britain has all doors open to immigration in this situation.

As I said, politicians and the illiterate majority of all journalists still keep pedalling the story that all immigrants are welcome as they will do the jobs the Brits themselves refuse to. But even they should realize that at some point overpopulation will lead to a total collapse not only of this country, but the world itself. Journalists keep praising India and Africa for their large breeding rates. How blind must one be to fail to see what is coming to all of us? Once again, that is especially important in light of the imminent climate crisis and global starvation. Yet, there is not a single sane voice in mainstream media addressing this.

The total **population of the world** in 1952 was **2.58 billion**. In 2024 it is 8.**16 and growing**. It is **3.2 times increase**.

In **1950**, there were **250 million people living in all of Africa**. Now there are as many of them as are in India and China - about **1500 million or 1.5 billion**. It is six-fold increase. And that number is going to grow. Neither in Africa, nor in India, nor in Pakistan, there will be any reductions of population in foreseeable future. And all of them will soon be in a great trouble because of food shortages and they will start to move to Europe. But Europe itself is overpopulated as it is...

In total there are some **4 billion people** in those **most overpopulated regions** of the world. In **European Union** itself there are already some **450 million people** living. Territory of European Union is around **4.2 million sq.km.** large. The average density there is similar to what **France** has, around **105 people per sq.km.**

Africa is around **30.3 million sq.km.** large. It is around **7.5 times larger than the EU**. Africa's density is around **50 people per sq.km.** Clearly, its density is slightly more than 2 times smaller compared to the EU. Of course, we have to exclude deserts and forests from this calculation, to get the correct density of Africa. But our politicians, as if on behalf of all of us, are ready to accept as many immigrants as are ready to come from those countries, despite enormous shortages of housing in most of EU countries already now, especially in England, where there is no land for any housing left anymore as it is. There is not enough land to feed those who are here already. And we don't have any sane politicians and journalists, and even scientists who would see these dangerous trends.

A proof for how forests are decreasing temperatures...

I recently read an article about the effects of forests on temperatures in the eastern part of the USA, published by **theguardian.com**. Next is the excerpt from that article. For some reason this is being ignored by everyone – politicians, scientists, climate activists, journalists...

> *Very cool: trees stalling effects of global heating in eastern US, study finds*
>
> **Vast reforestation a major reason for 'warming hole' across parts of US where temperatures have flatlined or cooled**
>
> <u>Oliver Milman, Sat 17 Feb 2024 10.00 GMT</u>
>
> *Trees provide innumerable benefits to the world, from food to shelter to oxygen, but researchers have now found their dramatic rebound in the eastern US has delivered a further, stunning feat – the curtailing of the soaring temperatures caused by the climate crisis.*
>
> *While the US, like the rest of the world, has heated up since industrial times due to the burning of fossil fuels (my remark – this claim is false), scientists have long been puzzled by a so-called "warming hole" over parts of the US south-east where temperatures have flatlined, or even cooled, despite the unmistakable broader warming trend.*

This is not the only known example when afforestation leads not only to a cooler climate, but it also leads to the return of life in general in the given area. Another such example has been shown in at least one territory in Africa, where everything was nearly turned into a desert. I don't remember the title of this documentary though, but there are many on this topic. They are on YouTube. Anyway... After having planted some trees there, in some 5-year time the grass started to grow, many animals and birds returned, and even humans started to grow their own food. The role of forests in our ecosystems is absolutely huge. And the same is true about their role in Relative Humidity and, by extension, in Climate Change. Yet, nobody is bothered about Deforestation.

What is the link between Deforestation and Climate Change?

Since Industrial Revolution, which is the time when the temperatures started to rise, **the world has lost around 20 million sq.km.** of ancient forests. They were cleared to free the land for agriculture. Whole **Russia is 17 mil.sq.km** large... So, **Russia and Kazakhstan together** would form the area of the lost forests in the world ever since. Of course, putting **together territories of China and USA** also have the same total area. As you can see, that is a huge territory even on a global scale. And the process of Deforestation is still ongoing...

So, what's the fuss about Deforestation, right?!

I will try to be as short as I can, and everyone can check the facts by themselves later. Once again - all this is also explained in my book – **WHERE DO THE UNIVERSE AND LIFE COME FROM**, as the second part of it addresses the potential end of life...

Turns out that one of the most important changes in our atmosphere, which leads to all climate problems, and especially to changes in rain patterns, are changes in air humidity. In short, **Relative Humidity** has been decreasing for ages, even though **Specific Humidity** has been increasing. In essence, that means that the air is getting drier and drier at any given temperatures, while the total amount of water in air is increasing. **Confused?** You should be, as are all the scientists. Still, they aren't talking about it as a problem and the true cause of climate change, even though it is these changes that directly affect the increase of temperatures, the longevity and severity of droughts and floods, and even the dangers of wildfires. But in this letter, I will explain all of that.

Before we do that, I would like to explain some facts. It is true that even though Relative Humidity is decreasing, the total or Specific Humidity is increasing. This happens because lower Relative Humidity leads to higher air temperatures from the same energy of the Sun. It can easily be proven by comparing wet and dry saunas. With the same amount of energy, a dry sauna will always reach significantly higher temperatures than a wet sauna. Not only will a wet sauna heat up slower, but it will also never reach the temperatures possible in a dry sauna. These facts alone prove that the humidity of air directly affects its temperatures. Namely, the drier the air, the higher the temperatures and less rain. **Conclusion:** Humidity might be the key factor affecting everything with respect to climate change. The amount of forests in a given neighbourhood definitely affects humidity!

How are trees affecting Relative Humidity and Climate Change in general?

Trees are moisturizing air through the process called "**transpiration**". I am sure it was taught to all of us at school, but most of us have forgotten many things from back then.

Wikipedia:

> *Water is necessary for plants but only a small amount of water taken up by the roots is used for growth and metabolism. The remaining* **97–99.5% is lost by transpiration**...

In my research I also learned that **one fully grown tree**, thanks to the process of **transpiration**, sprays around **40 tons of water** into the atmosphere every season... This is where I tried to do some calculations. From science data I estimated how many trees would have been in fully grown forests on a territory of **20 million of sq.km.** (the area that has been deforested since the industrial Revolution started), and the volume of water the air is losing every year because of that turned out to be mind-blowing. Turns out that our atmosphere annually isn't receiving an amount of water that would be similar to a pool with an area of **1000 km by 1000 km** and a **depth of 5 km**. This is roughly the surface area of Egypt. That is a huge amount of water our atmosphere isn't receiving every year because of the lost forests.

If this pool had a **surface area of the United Kingdom**, then the **depth of it would be around 28 km**. Even jets can hardly reach this altitude. Clearly, that must have a huge impact on the humidity of air all around the world. After all, we all share the same atmosphere, as it doesn't recognize borders. It also might be that water vapor and water from transpiration create microdroplets of different sizes. Together, they build up the total relative humidity. But now, when one of these 'humidity-affecting' factors has been heavily damaged, the average relative humidity is dropping all the time worldwide. And yes, we still carry on with worldwide deforestation at scary speeds, and we don't even talk about it. Deforestation is only mentioned in connection with the loss of habitats of many species, even though that is a huge problem too.

It will be a very sad story in human history if we, the humans, after correctly realizing that life on our planet, including the very existence of humans, is in jeopardy, yet focused on the wrong aspects to fix it. And this is exactly what we are currently doing. We are targeting CO2 emissions while the actual problem is Deforestation, which itself is caused by Overpopulation. This failure will lead to the extinction of humankind. We are losing a precious time to fix it. Meanwhile, Deforestation carries on as usual. I truly cannot understand how nobody can see these clear and obvious facts. And no, CO2 levels have no part in these predicaments at all.

The increase of CO2 levels is too small for any effect on climate.

The idea of CO2 levels being the main culprit of the climate crisis is complete nonsense. **CO2 levels have been 3 out of 10 thousand units of air** for ages. Over the last 200 years or so, **the level of CO2 has increased by one more CO2 unit out of 10 thousand**. Can this amount of CO2 increase lead to that dramatic decrease in Relative Humidity? I don't see how. After all, that is a tiny increase. On top of that, I already showed you the proof that Afforestation leads to a decrease in temperatures, and **the world has lost some 40% of its original territories of forests**. And yes, forests very directly affect the humidity, which directly affects the rain patterns. These changes are the most dangerous and devastating of all in this climate saga. Drier air, which is confirmed with lower relative humidity, also leads to higher wildfire risks.

The madness of human intervention in the processes of Nature.

Today, we hear a lot about **electric vehicles**, **renewable energy**, the **reduction of fertilizers**, and other **interventions in climate change** through methods like **cloud seeding**, **CO2 capturing**, and **spraying various substances into the atmosphere** to mitigate warming. We also see scientists queuing up to reject afforestation and depopulation, using different excuses. In reality, all these interventions in Natural processes could have unforeseen consequences for us all.

Later, I will explain how **cloud seeding** leads to **more droughts** and **higher temperatures**, similar to the effects of deforestation. In the UK, we need more food but have increasingly less land available for agriculture. Yet, the **British Prime Minister**, Kier Starmer, decides to

build houses on green belts to accommodate the country's **morbid overpopulation**, further reducing available land for forests...

It often seems to be the case that our world has been led by absolutely blind and deaf politicians and scientists, not to mention journalists. We are literally sleepwalking into an irreversible disaster. And nobody bothers to look up the facts, let alone explore them. I don't blame the likes of **Radio LBC** and the **BBC** for this, as they are paid to turn a blind eye and even to silence attempts by anyone else who raises these topics. But what about the rest of the world? Is there a single sane person left out there?

I want to be clear – **the "net zero" idea** is completely useless and won't solve a single climate problem. Afforestation, however, will solve all of them, but afforestation is impossible with swelling numbers of humans. Also, the "net zero" is virtually impossible to achieve. Yet, it will create a huge damage to prosperity and food security in whole world, bringing global starvation closer than it would come in a natural way.

Fighting combustion engines is like barking at the wrong tree. By doing that we are wasting the precious time needed to save the planet by planting more trees and stopping our breeding rates.

And don't listen to "experts", as they often are literally lying. The only thing to listen to are facts. If facts shown in this book are wrong, I cannot wait to hear you out.

PLEASE, PLEASE, PLEASE...

- If you find the facts in this book worthy of your attention and suitable for sharing with a wider population, please mention the book to others and spread the word!

What is wrong with Climate Change

In this chapter, I will provide you with some facts that prove how human activities are leading to the death of our planet. But the reasons for climate change are not what you expect them to be. In short, climate change is happening, and it is human-made, but it has little to nothing to do with CO2 emissions or the so-called "Greenhouse Effect." In fact, the idea of the Greenhouse Effect in the atmosphere is impossible to start with. All climate problems are caused by completely different changes in the world. I am writing about this because it would be a great shame if we later found out that we correctly realized there is a problem, and we were willing to do something about it, but failed because we have been barking up the wrong tree from day one. So, in this chapter, I will try to prove to you with very telling facts that there are way too many humans on this planet already, and that our consumption rates of woodlands are the most dangerous thing leading to all the changes in climate that we observe around us.

What is wrong with the claim about the <u>Greenhouse Effect!</u>

So, one of the most well-known claims of science on this topic is the so-called **Greenhouse Effect**. And I am not questioning the rising CO2 levels and their origins at all. After all, that is a clear fact. But these numbers do not prove the existence of any Greenhouse Effect.

What about rising temperatures then, right? Yes, temperatures are rising too, at least in most places and in general. But is it because of CO2 and the so-called Greenhouse Effect? That is the question I wanted to understand when I started to explore this topic. And, as I previously said, we better get it right, or we will end up wasting time and energy fighting something that has no part in these problems..

To understand the problem here, think about the greenhouse as we all know it. A greenhouse is a small and closed system. Its inside air is separated from the outer atmosphere by glass or plastic walls on all sides. This heavily reduces the movement of air inside it. But that means, when it heats up, it stays there. Also, the material of those outer walls provides much larger areas that heat up the surrounding inside air of the greenhouse. It is these walls that serve as additional heaters for the inside air.

What I wanted to point out here is the fact that greenhouses are places inside which the movement of air has been significantly limited and the surface areas that would be heating up this inside air have increased. This happens because the energy from the Sun heats up solid materials faster and to higher temperatures than the air. If any given amount of air is restricted to a certain area and cannot circulate in the atmosphere, then it heats up, attempting to match the temperatures of all those surrounding walls, which are hotter. And this, in short, is how the Greenhouse Effect works.

Clearly, nothing of that happens in the atmosphere. Even worse, the outer layers of the atmosphere are significantly cooling down. And that means the atmosphere of Earth is opposite of what would happen in a greenhouse...

When it comes to the atmosphere, there is no solid cover around the Earth that would heat up and limit the movement of air beneath it. Of course, if you believe in the Flat Earth theory, you might think that the Earth is indeed covered by a dome made of some unknown material. This would resemble a greenhouse. However, the Sun would be inside this dome, so it wouldn't affect the atmosphere in the same way a greenhouse does. Also, if such a dome existed, it would have been there forever, meaning its effects would have been constant. This applies to believers in the Flat Earth theory..

I already mentioned that the upper levels of our atmosphere are actually cooling down! This is important to know, especially with respect to claims about the Greenhouse Effect. After all, the upper layers of actual greenhouses do heat up, while the upper levels of our atmosphere are cooling down. That means the Sun's rays would become cooler because they move through those colder layers. But the temperatures on the surface of Earth are heating up anyway. So, what is going on?

Nasa.gov, Jun 30, 2021

NASA Satellites See Upper Atmosphere Cooling and Contracting Due to Climate Change

The sky isn't falling, but scientists have found that parts of the upper atmosphere are gradually contracting in response to rising human-made greenhouse gas emissions.

*Combined data from three **NASA** satellites have produced a long-term record that reveals **the mesosphere**, the layer of the atmosphere 30 to 50 miles above the surface, **is cooling and contracting**. Scientists have long predicted this effect of human-driven climate change, but it has been difficult to observe the trends over time.*

Some time ago, I mistakenly assumed that the levels of precipitation were also going down. My assumption was based on data from certain countries, where it was found that springs are increasingly becoming drier in terms of precipitation. However, that didn't describe the whole year. What I missed at the beginning of my research on this topic was the fact that the pattern of precipitation itself is changing. Precipitation used to be more frequent but with smaller volumes at each rainfall. Now, however, rain comes less frequently, but the volumes of water often are larger. And that, actually, is the real problem of Climate Change.

By the way, there indeed are places on Earth where there is less and less precipitation, as well as places with increased precipitation. Yet, the main problem is that, in most places on Earth, springs and early summers are suffering from reduced precipitation, while late summers and autumns suffer from increasing flood dangers.

And these patterns of precipitation are changing for a reason. Most likely, it is because of the **changed Relative Humidity**. But why is it changing? Why has it been going down? Answering this question might be the key to understanding the true causes of Climate Change. So, what are the options for culprits that could have caused the reduction of Relative Humidity, right?!

Types and essence of humidity!

Well, in order to move on with this topic of climate change, we have to understand how humidity is currently measured by science. After all, even most of the so-called climate activists are very poorly educated on these topics and have no clue about even the basic terms.

Wikipedia:

HUMIDITY

Humidity *is the concentration of water vapor present in the air. Water vapor, the gaseous state of water, is generally invisible to the human eye. Humidity indicates the likelihood for* **precipitation**, **dew**, *or* **fog** *to be present. Humidity depends on the temperature and pressure of the system of interest.*

...

Three primary measurements of humidity are widely employed: **absolute**, **relative**, *and* **specific**.

Absolute humidity *is expressed as either mass of water vapor per volume of moist air (in grams per cubic meter) or as mass of water vapor per mass of dry air (usually in grams per kilogram).*

Relative humidity, *often expressed as a percentage, indicates a present state of absolute humidity relative to a maximum humidity given the same temperature.*

Specific humidity *is the* **ratio** *of water vapor mass to total moist air parcel mass.*

> *Humidity plays an important role for surface life. For animal life dependent on **perspiration** (sweating) to regulate internal body temperature, high humidity impairs heat exchange efficiency by reducing the rate of moisture **evaporation** from skin surfaces.*

So, for the sake of this book we are mainly interested in **Relative Humidity** and **Specific Humidity**. And I would like to explain these two in my own words.

So, **Relative Humidity** is the actual moisture content of the air at any given moment compared to the maximum possible moisture content under the same conditions. At any given set of circumstances and specific temperatures, there is an average humidity level that is typical for those conditions. Normally, this humidity is always lower than the maximum possible humidity at that temperature. If 100% humidity is achieved under these conditions, it results in rain.

For instance, what is considered 100% humidity at a temperature of +10°C would only be about 80% humidity at +13°C. This means that if the air temperature is rising, rain is less likely. However, if the air cools from +13°C to +10°C, and the humidity at +13°C was 80%, then upon reaching +10°C, the relative humidity for this temperature will become 100% and could lead to rain.

Let's go through it all one more time.

If somebody tells you that the relative humidity at a given temperature is 50%, it means these 50% are relative to the total possible humidity of air at that particular temperature. If the temperature rises, then the same amount of water in the air might represent, say, 30% for the new temperature. And yes, Relative Humidity used to stay at a certain average level at any given temperature. But now, it has been in decline for many decades due to changes in the climate.

Specific Humidity is simply the actual amount of water vapor in the air at any given moment, regardless of other conditions. It is expressed in units of weight. Specifically, it can be stated how many grams of water there are per unit of air. Essentially, it represents the total amount of water in the air at any given time. According to science, this measurement is increasing.

Sounds like some kind of contradiction here, right? After all, the air is becoming drier even though the total amount of water in the air is increasing. The thing is—Relative Humidity is indeed declining while Specific Humidity is increasing, simply because average temperatures are rising. When the temperature of the air increases by 1 degree, it can hold 7% more water. And then the air is actively trying to attract that water from wherever it can get its hands on it.

Now, let's take a look at what professionals say about the changes in humidity levels.

Changes of humidity levels cause a parados, according to **Met Office**. Borrowed from **www.weforum.org**

> ### *Humidity Paradox*
>
> *The key reasons for this apparent paradox are two-fold: the Earth is warming, and warmer air can hold more water vapour.*
>
> *The atmosphere, land and oceans **are all warming**. First, this means that more water is being evaporated from the Earth's surface. Second, more water can – and is – being held in the air as a gas. As the chart below shows, the increase in specific humidity is occurring over both the land (green line) and the oceans (blue).*

Next, we are going to look at the changes in Specific and Relative Humidity. We will look at Specific (or total) Humidity first.

Changes of Specific (total) Humidity over a 30-year period.

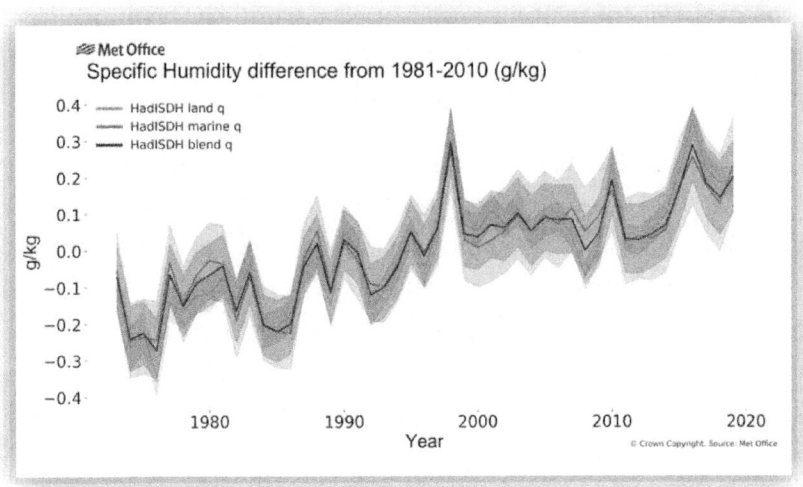

Global time series of annual average specific humidity for the land (green line), ocean (blue) and global average (dark blue), relative to 1981-2010. Image: Met Office Climate Dashboard

This image shows the decrease in Relative Humidity.

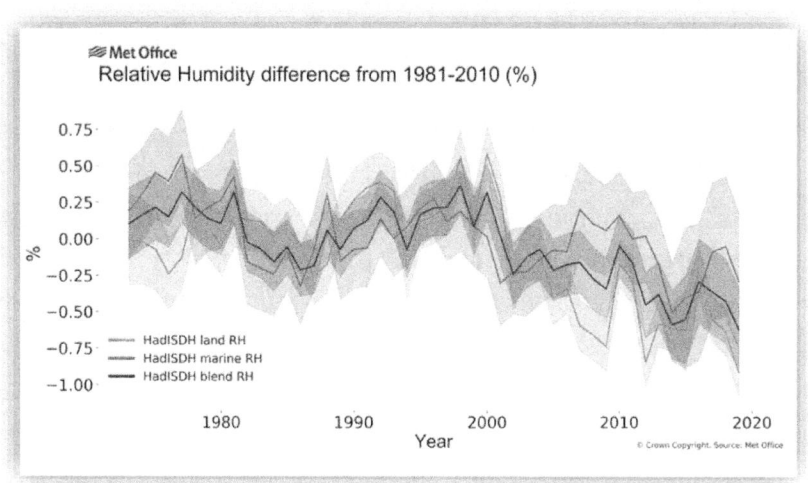

From the same article:

https://www.weforum.org/agenda/2020/12/climate-change-humidity-paradox/

> According to the **Clausius-Clapeyron equation**, the air can generally hold around **7%** more moisture for every 1C of temperature rise. Therefore, for relative humidity to stay the same under 1C of warming, the moisture content in the air also needs to increase by 7%.
>
> In theory, if there are no limiting factors, then this is the rate of increase we would expect to see. However, the real world does have limiting factors – and so relative humidity is decreasing.
>
> The Earth's land surface has been **warming faster** than the oceans over the past few decades. But, while the oceans contain an inexhaustible supply of water to be evaporated, the same is not the case for land.

> *In fact, we know that most of the water vapour over land actually originates from evaporation over oceans.* This moist air is moved around the globe thanks to the atmospheric circulation and some then flows over land.
>
> The slower warming of the oceans means that there has not been enough moisture evaporated into – and then held in – the air above the oceans to keep pace with the **rising temperatures over land**. This means that the air is not as saturated as it was and – as the previous chart shows – relative humidity has decreased.

Unfortunately, there are still too many unknown factors in this story. For instance, the formation of clouds is not yet fully understood by science. Science also fails to recognise the role forests play in the planet's humidity, despite some very strong evidence supporting this idea.

In the previous quote from the Met Office, we learned that my claim about water heating up more slowly and slowing down the heating process of our planet is correct. After all, why would the oceans heat up more slowly? And guess what? – Relative Humidity is also decreasing above the oceans...

This is where I could explain the huge role forests play in global humidity and rainfall patterns, but there are still some things that need to be explored before we move on to that question.

***

The thing is – and I've already mentioned this several times in this book – **water regulates temperatures**. I also said that a wet sauna will never reach the same temperatures as a dry sauna with the same amount of energy. So, these facts indirectly prove that the drier the air, the higher the temperatures it will reach with the same amount of energy. And since we can safely assume that the Sun provides the same amount of energy on average, it could be that these higher temperatures on Earth have been reached because the air is getting drier than it used to be. So, if this is true, and I believe it is, we need to figure out what could have led to the air becoming drier, right?

Turns out, there is one factor that should indeed be affecting the humidity before temperatures or CO2 levels change. In fact, this factor affects both temperatures and CO2 levels. And that factor is deforestation.

Before we address that, let's take a look at the CO2 emissions saga.

The fake news about the role of CO2 emissions in climate change

So, let's take a closer look at CO2 itself and its possible role in climate change. After all, it has changed over the last 200+ years, and the scientific community insists that it is the main, and possibly the only, culprit of climate change. Now I will do my best to show you that this claim is wrong.

When I ask climate activists about the CO2 levels in the atmosphere, they rarely know much about these numbers. If you're lucky, they'll know that CO2 levels have risen from **300 (or 280) ppm** to around **400 (or 420) ppm**. Well, when presented like this, it seems like a fairly big jump, right? And **"ppm"** stands for **parts per million**. Is it any clearer now? No? Trust me, it's really important to understand these numbers. But such presentation doesn't help it.

Wikipedia:

> In **science** and **engineering**, the **parts-per notation** is a set of pseudo-units to describe small values of miscellaneous **dimensionless quantities**, e.g., **mole fraction** or **mass fraction**. Since these **fractions** are quantity-per-quantity measures, they are pure numbers with no associated **units of measurement**. Commonly used are **parts-per-million (ppm,** 10^{-6}**),**...
>
> ...
>
> This notation is not part of the **International System of Units** (SI) system, and its meaning is ambiguous.

As you can see, the abbreviation **'ppn'** isn't even a specific classification. It's just a concept behind such ways of describing things. And knowing that **'ppm'** means **parts per million** doesn't help us understand the actual ratio at all. However, we can calculate the size of this 'ppm' by comparing it to its percentage equivalent. So, **400 ppm** is the same as **0.04%** of the given volume.

So, to be clear, the actual increase in CO2 in the world (from **0.03% to 0.04%) is around 0.01%.** Expressed in other way, this means the increase is roughly **one ten-thousandth** (!!!) of the atmosphere... Ask yourself – can this increase have contributed to all the changes in our climate? Can the change of such a tiny scale have raised the temperature by 1.5 degrees Celsius? I don't think so! Do you even know how much one ten-thousandths is? Imagine a distance of 10 meters. 10 meters are 10 thousand millimetres. So, if you added just one millimetre to this distance, you would have the same scale of change. It is miserably tiny.

Another visualisation of how much **1/10'000dth** is can be seen in the next image... That is a two-dimensional representation of it. Yes, that dark dot shows the volume of **1/10'000dth** compared to the size of that square. Not that much, eye?

Wikipedia:

Carbon Dioxide in Earth's Atmosphere

*The current global average concentration of CO_2 in the atmosphere is (0.04%) 421 **ppm** as of May 2022. This is an increase of 50% since the start of the **Industrial Revolution**,* up from 280 ppm during the 10,000 years prior to the mid-18th century.

At this point, it is important to be crystal clear about when the industrial Revolution started.

Wikipedia:

> The **Industrial Revolution** was a period of global transition of **human economy** towards more efficient and stable manufacturing processes that succeeded the **Agricultural Revolution**, starting from Great Britain, **continental Europe**, and the United States, that occurred during the period <u>from around **1760** to about **1820–1840**</u>.

So, as you can see, the **Industrial Revolution** has been around for roughly **200 to 260 years**. During this time, the world has witnessed an **increase** in **human population** and **deforestation** to levels previously unheard of. These numbers have changed far more than CO2 levels, and ignoring them would be a crime against the facts.

According to '**Worldometers**', in **1760 (265** years ago**)** there were only around **770 million** people in the whole world.

Here is the link to those numbers:

https://www.worldometers.info/world-population/world-population-by-year/

Nowadays, China and India alone have twice that number each. Even **in 1970**, there were only around **4 billion** people. Now, 55 years later, we have double that number. Try comparing the change in these numbers with the changes in CO2 levels. And I haven't even begun to discuss the levels of deforestation, which really picked up starting with the Industrial Revolution.

Interesting to know – *an increase in CO2 should lead to fewer wildfires, as it reduces the amount of oxygen in the air, which is needed for the chemical reaction known as fire. But when you say this to* **'CO2 haters,'** *they will tell you that the amount is far too small to reduce wildfires. At the same time, they have no problem believing that these same tiny CO2 levels significantly affect our climate. Humidity, on the other hand, if reduced, would indeed help wildfires, as it leads to drier air. So, it's a no-brainer to determine which of them would lead to more problems when it comes to climate change. But if that's true for wildfires, maybe it's reasonable to consider that, in the same way, lower humidity is responsible for higher temperatures on Earth. The only thing we need to work out at this point is what causes the reduction in humidity and why it still counts as a reduction, even if the Specific or total humidity has increased*

The next image (a chart from **www.washingtonpost.com**) is showing how "CO2 haters" are manipulating with the numbers of CO2. Can you spot the problem?

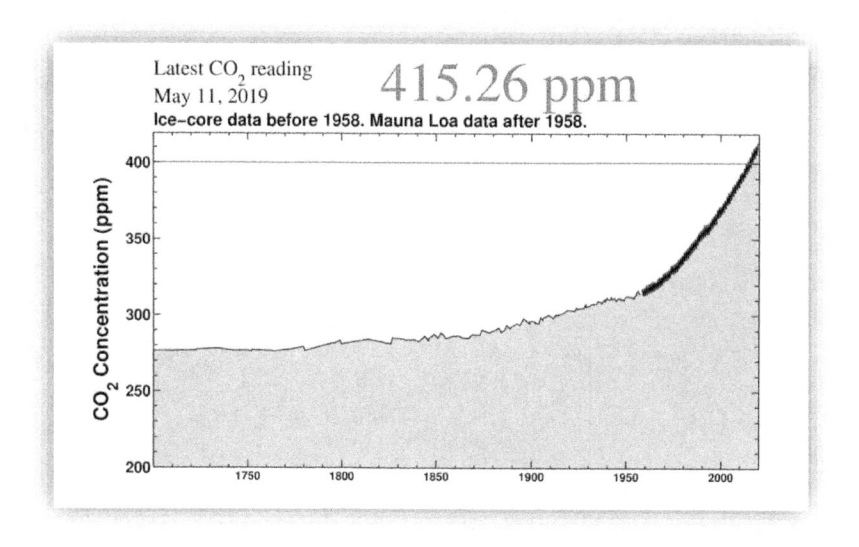

Here, you should instantly realise (if you're trained in spotting manipulations) that all images depicting the changes in CO2 levels are missing the bottom 200 units in these charts. **What's the fuss about it?**

When you look at the previous chart as it is, you're given the **impression that CO2 levels have doubled since 1950**. By the way, it was around that time, 75 years ago, when temperatures and CO2 levels really began to rise. Let's remember that **in 1950, there were only 2.5 billion people on this planet.** Yet, even since then, CO2 levels have increased by around 50%. However, on this chart, it seems that CO2 levels have doubled over the last 75 years. You may not realise it, but the reader is meant to perceive this increase as being larger than it actually is. **That's a form of deception.** Meanwhile, **the human population has tripled** during the same last 75 years, and nobody seems to be bothered about that.

Even though many will be aware of the missing part in the chart, it will still leave a strong impression on the reader's subconscious. Make no mistake – these things are created deliberately and are meant to deceive your perception. But that means someone is deliberately trying to manipulate you.

Now that the size of CO2 levels and some of the manipulations involved in their representation are clear, we can move on to why forests are important to global ecosystems.

JURIS BOGDANOVS

Transpiration and the importance of trees in humidity levels

Before we move on to the question of deforestation, I must reveal one very important detail about plants that has been heavily overlooked by science when it comes to climate change. That detail is **transpiration**.

Wikipedia:

> **Transpiration** *is the process of* **water** *movement through a* **plant** *and its* **evaporation** *from aerial parts, such as* **leaves, stems,** *and* **flowers**. *Water is necessary for plants but only a small amount of water taken up by the roots is used for growth and metabolism. The remaining* **97–99.5%** *is lost by transpiration and* **guttation.**

In essence, plants only keep around **0.5 to 3%** of all the water they extract from soil. The rest of it they spray out in the atmosphere. And this fact could be the most important in all this narrative about the Climate Change completely trumping effects of changing CO2 levels.

I want you to realise that this function of plants means that forests could be doing the same thing that water vapour from oceans does – it is moisturising the atmosphere. On top of that, there is a good chance that water from plants is different from water vapour from seas. It's possible that these two mechanisms are both needed together to maintain healthy water cycles on planet. I have already mentioned that science still cannot explain with certainty how clouds form. Who knows, maybe the world of plants is the most important part of it! And that would mean the fewer forests there are, the fewer clouds there are as well. But clouds provide both shade and rain...

The next question we should naturally ask is this: how much water might a large tree process during a given period of time? After all, even if they release into the atmosphere a staggering 97 to 99% of all the water they extract, perhaps it's still based on a relatively small total volume. As it turns out, they actually process an incredible amount of water...

The next quote comes from the **Purdue University's** (USA) website: **https://www.purdue.edu**

> **Purdue Landscape Report: How do trees use water?**
>
> Trees can absorb between **10 and 150 gallons of water daily**, yet of all the water absorbed by plants, less than 5% remains in the plant for growth. They rely on available water in the soil to "rehydrate" during the night-time hours, replacing the water loss during the daytime hours.
>
> The second process is the interception of water by the surfaces of leaves, branches and trunks during rainfall, and its following evaporation. Together, these two processes are often referred to as evapotranspiration. Both transpiration and evaporation are strongly affected by the amount of sunlight, the temperature and humidity of the air, as well as wind speed as trees turn water into mist when it **releases** nearly **95%** of the water it absorbs.

As you can see, this article states that trees process between 10 to 150 gallons of water DAILY... Since this university is located in the USA, we have to assume that those are US gallons they are using here. British gallons are larger than American ones.

www.theunitconverter.com

> **Gallons (UK) :** A gallon (UK) is a unit of volume, which is commonly used in the United Kingdom and semi-officially within Canada. It is defined as **4.54609 liters** distinguished from the **United States (liquid) gallon (≈ 3.79 L)**.

According to the previous quote, **10 to 50 gallons** would represent around **38 to 190 litres of water daily**! And that is indeed a staggering amount. So, if each tree does this every day, it's no wonder that water cycles (and relative humidity) have been affected all over the world after we have annihilated more than **20 million square kilometres** of forests and heavily damaged, as I will explain later, many of the remaining ones.

By the way, have you ever thought about this question: why did we used to have so much rain in autumn? Of course, it still happens, but on a somewhat smaller scale, and when it rains, it pours...

The thing is, in regions closer to the poles, trees hibernate during winter and only produce leaves (which they use for transpiration) in summer. Every summer, these trees release so much moisture into the air that it leads not only to very high relative humidity, but also to lower temperatures due to the large volumes of water in the air. I've explained before that higher humidity leads to lower temperatures with the same amount of energy from the Sun. But since in autumn there is much more moisture in the air, and temperatures begin to drop also due to shorter days, it leads to very high relative humidity, exactly because of the temperature drop. And that means rain.

So, slight cooling of the atmosphere due to reduced temperatures and shorter days, combined with high relative humidity, leads to an increase in rainfall. The rain will continue as long as temperatures keep dropping, simply because at lower temperatures, the air can hold less moisture. Since summers are hotter and trees produce a lot of moisture during them, the air becomes very saturated with water, which inevitably leads to rain as soon as temperatures start to drop.

Of course, because temperatures are constantly changing, rain is quite frequent when there is high relative humidity in the air. And frequent but light rain is very beneficial. High relative humidity also helps to control temperature fluctuations within smaller ranges. It is large temperature changes that lead to floods. And drier air leads to greater temperature fluctuations...

Another thing to keep in mind, with respect to these processes, is that it always takes time for air humidity to change on a global scale. Namely, even when we are levelling forests at staggering rates, the effects of reduced humidity in the air could lag behind for several decades. This means that the effects of today's deforestation might only become apparent after several years, but we will definitely see them. So, if we already recognise that there is a huge problem with the climate, and if it is indeed mainly due to deforestation, then no **'zero CO2'** policies will help, even if we achieved them tomorrow at dinner time.

The biggest issue with respect to this story is that at the **COP26 Climate Conference**, more than **100 world leaders promised** to end and begin **reversing deforestation by 2030**. But even now, we know that the planet is already in a desperate state, and even if we started afforestation today, we would still pay the price for areas that have already been deforested, as it takes several years for positive changes to begin manifesting. The 2030 deadline is clearly not enough! And politicians don't even take it seriously... It's more like their bla, bla, bla, but with no intention to actually address this problem.

Politicians and scientists clearly have no clue about what is happening. They are greatly underestimating the role of deforestation in climate change and how to address it, while they are heavily overestimating the role of CO2 emissions in climate change. And there is nothing that would make them do anything...

The next image is from the **USDA** – U.S. DEPARTMENT OF AGRICUTURE/ **Forest Service**

> How much water does a tree drink in a day?
>
> HOW MUCH WATER DOES A TREE DRINK? A healthy 100-foot-tall tree has about 200,000 leaves. A tree this size can take **11,000 gallons** of water from the soil and release it into the air again, as oxygen and water vapor, in a single growing season.
>
> https://www.fs.usda.gov › Internet
> Water & Forests

So, **98% of 11'000 US Gallons** is **10'780**. Converted into litres it gives us a staggering **41'000 litres**. And that is only from one fully grown tree... Tell me, if you think that levelling areas of forests that represent around **One Third** of whole landmasses of our planet would have no impact on our climate if every single fully grown tree was spraying such a huge amount of water into our atmosphere?

Wikipedia:

> *One liter of water has a mass of almost exactly one kilogram when measured at its maximal density, which occurs at about 4 °C.*

This means, **41'000 litres** are the same as **41 metrical ton**...

Famously, America is a home of giant sequoias...

> How much water do oak trees drink a day?
>
> about 100 gallons
>
> 8. A large oak tree can consume about **100 gallons** of water per day, and a giant sequoia can drink up to 500 gallons daily.
>
> h https://www.hvoss.org.uk › media

This is UK's website. So, the gallon here would be equivalent to 4.5 litters. That means, one oak tree processes around **450 litres** of water daily, while giant sequoia would do **2250 litres**... It is **2.2 tons** of water every day...

From website: https://www.advnture.com/features/giant-sequoias

> **What is a sequoia tree?**
>
> *Sequoia trees are coniferous evergreen trees that are a member of the Cupressaceae family of trees, better known as the cypress family, and are the sole living species in the genus sequoiadendron. These hulking trees only grow naturally in a small stretch about 250 miles along the western slope of northern California's Sierra Nevada Mountains, mostly between 5,000 and 7,000 feet in elevation.*

Well, these trees clearly need special conditions and grow only in special places. However, their contribution to moisturizing the atmosphere is enormous. This also shows us that the size of the tree, or the total green mass of its leaves, also matters. Very soon I will explain to you in more details how exactly that is important with respect to this story.

Scientists don't know how clouds are formed

Before we move on, I would like to share something else with you!

This story is a daring speculation, but you will see that it is a logical assumption too! *– So, it could be that clouds only form from the water droplets created by plants! It also could be that plants become like* **depositories of moisture and water** *above the landmass of Earth. But that would mean that the total mass of green leaves of plants on Earth is very important. It could be too small or even too large...* ***To understand this hypothesis of mine, look at the next image.***

So, in essence (according to this hypothesis), there are two sources of moisture in atmosphere – **evaporation** from open waters, and **transpiration** from plants. They both contribute and, most likely, cooperate in creating the total Relative Humidity. And since the sheer volume of plants on Earth is diminishing at astonishing rates, no wonder that the air is becoming dryer.

Higher Relative Humidity would lead to more frequent but less massive rainfalls. Higher Humidity would also keep the air slightly cooler on hot days and slightly warmer on cold days. And humidity created by plants might be very, very important in **formation of clouds** as it might be creating smaller droplets of water than water evaporation does. That would lead to this moisture being able to move up higher than the one created by water vapor. And this would also explain how the two types of moisture are not causing an instant rain because of higher actual Relative Humidity created by them. Possibly, each of them on their own can only achieve a certain level of Relative Humidity. You have to admit that this idea would indeed explain the changes in humidity, temperatures, rain patterns, etc.

Also, since the plants would be keeping the atmosphere around them moister, and science has firmly confirmed that plants do just that (as quoted previously) by spraying up to 99% of all the absorbed water back into air, then we can safely speculate that actions of plants become like mechanisms which maintain a higher moisture above the landmass of Earth. And it could be that the same moisture created by plants makes Relative Humidity higher also above the oceans. But all that taken together means one thing - the total amount of the green mass of plants on Earth is very important for the levels of humidity and climate. Later I will explain to you that our Earth, very likely, has could have lost up to 80% of all the green mass that the world of plants used to have some 400 years ago.

To summarise the process of water being trapped above the landmass by plants! - The water that evaporates from seas occasionally falls on the land in the form of rain. And if there are plants, they capture it and start to create a very moist microclimate all-around of them. The humidity created by plants coexist with the humidity created by the water vapor, and in this way they both provide a level of Relative Humidity that is higher than they would have achieved on their own. This higher humidity leads to more frequent rain, ensuring that the trapped water remains above the landmass. But that means – over time more and more water from seas would be captured above the land and not only in the air. It would also lead to more moist soil and more healthy cycles of water inside of Earth. The excess water wouldn't cause floods as it would come in smaller portions, would be better absorbed by the wet soil, and leave the land via rivers, which would be full of water all the time.

And all this healthy water cycle would be achieved and sustained by the green mass of plants on Earth. So, in this way, the world of plants would be responsible for having captured larger volumes of drinking water and keeping them above the land. Effectively, if the world had a healthy water cycles, then we would never run out of drinking water. And to have these healthy water cycles, the volume of total green mass of plants is utterly important.

So, if anything of this is true, then plants (or lack of them) are a big part of the patterns of rain-falls or precipitation and even temperatures above the Earth due levels of humidity. If that is clear, we can move on. And the next part of the story is about the levels of Deforestation on Earth started from Industrial Revolution. Yes, deforestation started some time before it. Unfortunately, "CO2 haters" are bringing up this moment in history as the starting point for Climate Change, so this is why we too are going to stick to it.

The levels and role of deforestation

200 years of deforestation. Borrowed from:

https://rainforests.mongabay.com/general_tables.htm

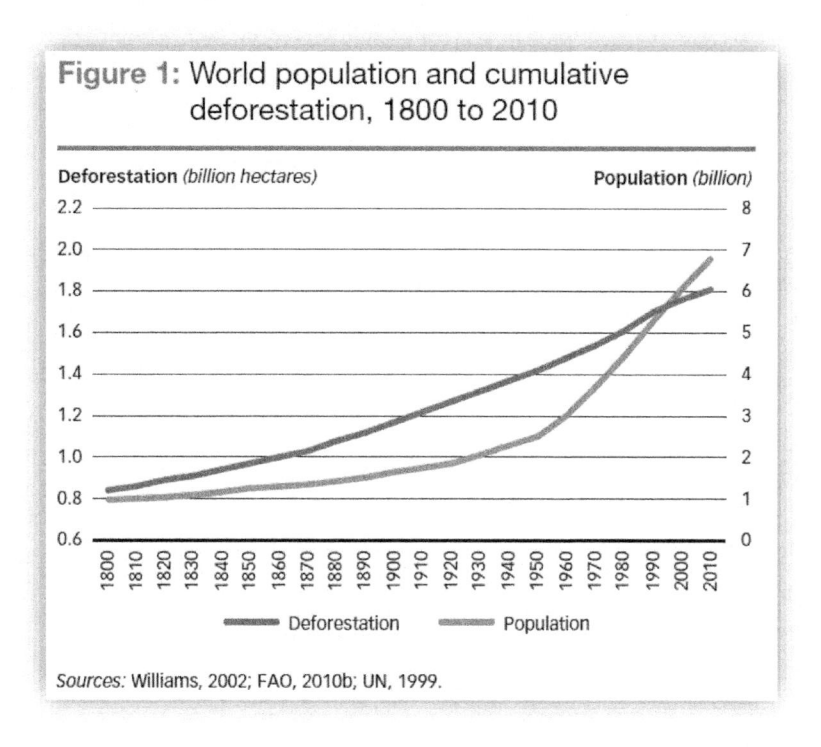

Figure 1: World population and cumulative deforestation, 1800 to 2010

Deforestation (billion hectares) / Population (billion)

Sources: Williams, 2002; FAO, 2010b; UN, 1999.

As you can see, these figures indeed have been changing way more that **CO2 level, which only increased by one ten thousandth** over this period. Pay attention to the fact that there appears to be a very direct corelation between the growth of population and deforestation. Also, pay attention to the fact that these numbers have grown way more than CO2 levels have increased. So, ask yourself - why everyone is so focused on CO2 emissions and only slightly addressing the numbers of Deforestation and Overpopulation? Where is that self-glorifying science community that prises itself for being impartial to facts? And why are all these other facts so overlooked when it comes to Climate Change? After all, most scientists even keep saying that there is not enough people on this world, and Deforestation is only bad because it affects biodiversity. Clearly, they know little to nothing about how climate works and what affects it.

The next chart shows the levels of Deforestation globally over the last 3 centuries or so. It comes from the website:

From: **https://rainforests.mongabay.com/general_tables.htm**

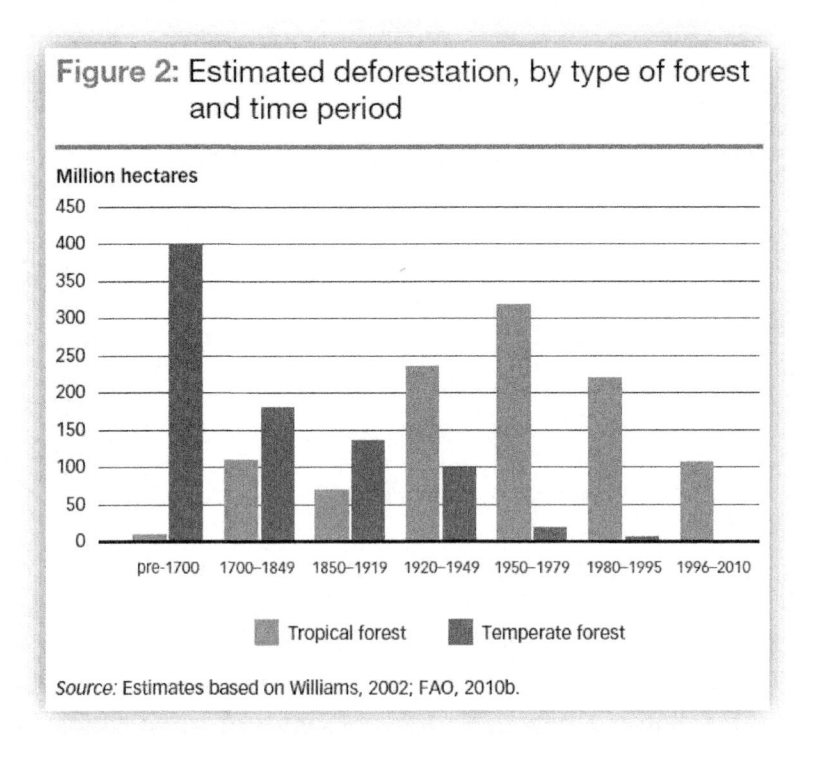

Figure 2: Estimated deforestation, by type of forest and time period

Source: Estimates based on Williams, 2002; FAO, 2010b.

I did some quick calculations here, and the total territory of lost forests is around **19 million square kilometres** over the last 300 years. It is also important to mention that some time ago I read an article about significant underreporting of lost woodlands in a large number of countries, as nobody wants to be told of and do anything about it. This is why countries literally cook the books when addressing Deforestation, and the actual levels of it might be way bigger. For this reason, I think it is only fair if we round this number up and say that the world has lost at least **20 million square kilometres** of forests. Do you even know how much it is on the map of the world? Well, the area of the USA or China are around 10 million square kilometres each. Basically, forests have lost territory that is similar to both of these countries taken together. You can also compare it with the whole Russia and Kazakhstan taken together. Yes, these areas are just mind-blowingly huge. But science keeps pedalling the question of the **CO_2 emissions**, which have risen by only **1/10'000** of atmosphere...

Well, according to science, the world has lost around 45% of the forests it used to have at some point before the Industrial Revolution. In reality, as I mentioned it previously, these numbers are very likely to have been heavily underreported. Again, it is only fair to assume that the Earth has lost at least **50%** of its former forest areas. And even that is only part of the problem with underreporting...

Let's take a look at the next image that will explain how and why Deforestation of our world might be the only true problem leading to the current Climate Change.

In this image you can see several things that affect the climate on Earth and, effectively, lead to changes in temperatures all over the globe along with reduced Relative Humidity. The main problem here is that both sides of this image would be shown as woodlands in statistics. In first part of this drawing you can see large trees that create large shadows under them. On top of that, I created a dotted area around these trees that represents the field of higher humidity created by the mass of green leaves of these trees. As I said it previously, water reduces the impact of Sunrays when they reach the surface of Earth. That means, both these phenomena (larger shadow areas and higher humidity) lead to lower temperatures on the globe in total. And **20 million square kilometres** of lost forests made out of huge trees definitely must have affected the climate all around the world.

On the other side of this drawing you can see the same forest being cut down, and new saplings having emerged. Clearly, their shadows are much smaller and so are their "**moisturizing-the-air**" capacity. Yet, on the paper both of these areas are described as forests. And that leads to another problem – what if most of those forests that we have been left with today, and which are described as forests on the paper, are actually recovering forests that cannot provide 10% of moisture levels and size of shadow compared to what adult forests did?! That would mean that the world could have lost much more of the total green mass of plants than those 50% that science admits as the lost forest areas. As I said previously, it wouldn't surprise me at all if the total green mass of plants lost is closer to some 80%.

It is very sad to think about these lost territories of forests and how they are underestimated by science and everyone, really. Clearly, the air is becoming dryer all over the world and we are already starting to suffer consequences of that. And this trend keeps rapidly advancing. Namely, everything is drying out. Look at the next image.

Here you can see the cracks in the soil. This image was taken in Eastern England, in June of 2023. The problem is - these cracks have been there for some 3 months now. Basically, they have been there for the whole spring. And you can see all fields in the neighbourhood being in the same state. Yet, cutting the grass nearly to the ground is not helping at all, as the grass is also a plant and also is moisturizing the air to certain extent. But if it is cut, it cannot do this anymore at all. So, yes, cutting our lawns too often and too low is also contributing to drier and hotter climate conditions.

Now, in the next image, take a look at the broader area of where the previous image was taken. Yes, all this area is covered in these cracks. And so are absolutely all other fields in the neighbourhood. Only some 5 years ago this wasn't happening. But that indicates – the climate changes are very rapidly advancing... And cracks in soil are extremely dangerous. Why?

The thing is – since the air has become drier, we can describe it as being "**thirsty for water**"!!! That means, air attracts any water it can get its hands on. Previously, when the Relative Humidity was high, the air wasn't doing it or did it at much lesser scale, the soil had enough moisture throughout the year and there were no cracks. Now, when drying up caused these cracks to appear, the air instantly gained access to deeper levels of soil and, for that reason, is draining its humidity at faster speed. When the rain comes, it won't be able to replace the lost levels of humidity in soil. This is why all types of corps are in danger. The dry air is killing the presence of water in soil. But no plants can live without the water.

Strangely, when you would talk to scientists and climate activists, they will totally fail to see this. You might ask them – Is the Relative Humidity reducing? And they would say – yes! Ask them again – Are the trees spraying significant amount of water in atmosphere? And they would say – yes! Ask them again – Have we lost 20 million sq. km (50%) of forests worldwide? And they would say – yes! Ask them again – What do you think is the true reason for this drying up and climate change? And they would say – **CO2**! How???

The role of clouds in climate change

Now, for a short moment, I would like to return to the formation of clouds and the role of clouds in Climate Change.

Obviously, this has everything to do with Deforestation too. Namely, the amount of clouds seems to be changing too. As I previously said, formation of clouds is still a very unsettled science. On top of that, it is close to impossible to work out the actual changes in clouds, like the changes of their thickness and sizes. For that reason, we cannot say anything with 100% certainty here. However, there are some research that indicates, that my hypothesis might be correct. But before looking at that, look at this image.

As you can see, the size of clouds matters. Clouds reduce the heating up of air as they create vast areas of shadow under them. The more there are clouds, and the thicker they are, the cooler the world under them. And together with the shadow areas caused by forests, which are cooler still than under the clouds, the total percentage of atmosphere that is made cooler in these shadows would be fairly large to leave an impact. After all, this cooler part of atmosphere interacts with the rest of it bringing down the total average temperatures. If you have ever been in your life in forests, you will definitely know how much cooler it is in forests compared to outside of them. On some years in Latvia we were able to find snow under some fir trees in the middle of May, but that was all those years ago, while the rest of the land was in full blossoms and really hot for weeks. Clearly, larger shadow areas and thicker clouds lead to cooler planet too, as do shadows from large areas of Virgin Forests. Only that we have annihilated some 50% of them for good. And that has reduced the sizes of clouds too.

Unfortunately, only very recently scientists started to realise that there might be a link between the clouds and temperatures on Earth. Only recently they started to say that clouds (which basically is a field with high humidity), is cooling down Earth instead of "trapping the Sunrays", which would lead to heating up. Yet even then they are still suggesting that some clouds do one thing, while the others achieve a complete opposite. Don't ask me how they managed to come to this conclusion, as that simply cannot be true ever. Please, read what scientists think about the clouds and their role in Climate Change in this **Washington Post** article.

The Washington Post, 12th December 2022, by Shannon Osaka

One of climate change's great mysteries is finally being solved

Scientists are beginning to understand whether clouds are a friend or enemy of climate change

For over a decade, the largest scientific uncertainty about how the planet will respond to warming temperatures hasn't come from how much carbon dioxide will be soaked up by the ocean or absorbed by the trees. It comes, instead, from clouds.

The fluffy, whimsical collections of water droplets floating in the air have, for some time, confounded climate scientists and models alike. Scientists have long known that depending on how clouds respond to warming temperatures, the world could become even warmer or a little bit cooler. They just haven't known which.

But in the past few years, scientists have begun to nail down exactly how clouds will change shape and location in the rapidly warming world. The result is good news for science — but not good news for humanity.

*"We've found evidence of the amplifying impact of clouds on global warming," said **Paulo Ceppi**, a climate scientist at **Imperial College London**.*

In reality, what Dr Ceppi here said is a 100% Confirmational Bias. I already explained it in this book that waters heat up and cool down slower than air. In general, this fact itself means nothing. But if somebody observes and concentrates only on one of these processes, in this case on the slower cooling, then using only it he can declare that clouds lead to warmer climate. But that wouldn't be true at all.

...continuation of the article...

> Scientists have long known that clouds have two primary influences on the global climate. First, clouds are reflective — their white surfaces reflect the sun's rays away from Earth, creating a cooling effect. (If the planet were suddenly devoid of these fluffy parasols, the planet would be roughly **five times hotter** than even the most disastrous global warming projections.) But clouds also create a warming effect — certain types of clouds insulate the Earth's radiation, keeping the planet warm much like carbon dioxide released from the burning of fossil fuels.

I will never understand these claims about radiation (and with that they mean also higher temperatures) being trapped inside the atmosphere. It is just impossible. When you remove the source of heat, then the substances instantly start to cool down as they resisted that warming to start with. Nothing is anywhere trapped ever. Also, higher temperatures during the day due to drier air lead to faster collapse and to lower temperatures at night.

www.livescience.com/why-do-deserts-get-cold-at-night.html

> If you're taking a day trip to the **Sahara Desert in North Africa,** you're going to want to bring a lot of water and plenty of sunscreen. But if you're planning to stay the night, then you better bring a snug sleeping bag, too.
>
> That's because temperatures in the Sahara can plummet once the sun sets, from an average high of **100 degrees** Fahrenheit **(38 degrees Celsius)** during the day to an average low of **25 degrees** Fahrenheit **(minus 4 degrees Celsius)** during the night, **according to NASA.**

The air over deserts is very dry. The lack of moisture allows the temperatures to fluctuate a lot. And because the air is becoming drier all over the world, so it is over deserts too. But that means, it allows the wind to spread the sand much easier. Yes, high humidity would stop deserts spreading. Another side effect of changes in humidity. And we are very close to being beyond that line after which our activities will be irreversible...

Back to that Washington Post article...

> Which effect is stronger depends on the type of cloud. Cirrus clouds — high, wispy clouds visible in the distant atmosphere on relatively clear days — absorb and trap more radiation, warming the Earth. Stratus or stratocumulus clouds — plump, fluffy clouds that often hover over the ocean on overcast days — reflect more sunlight, cooling the Earth.
>
> How exactly those two factors will balance out as the world warms has been uncertain. That's mostly because, even though clouds can look gigantic — when you are flying through them in a plane or looking up at them from the ground — they form at microscopic levels, when water vapor condenses around a particle of dust or a droplet. As a result, they are essentially impossible to model in the standard big climate models. (Clouds form at the micrometer level, while the models that most climate scientists use separate the world into blocks hundreds of kilometers in width.)
>
> We have a really tough time simulating with any fidelity how clouds actually behave in the real world," said **Timothy Myers**, an atmospheric scientist at the **University of Colorado**, Boulder.

But in recent years, scientists have gained increasing clarity on what will happen — and what is already happening — to clouds as the planet warms.

First, the high, wispy cirrus clouds that trap the Earth's radiation are expected to shift upward in the atmosphere, to lower temperature zones. Thanks to a complicated relationship between clouds and the radiation of the Earth, that will increase the amount of radiation that the cirrus clouds trap in the atmosphere. "When they rise, their greenhouse effect, or warming effect, on the Earth tends to increase," Myers said.

*That result has been known for about a decade and indicates that clouds are likely to amplify global warming. But just in the past few years, researchers have also discovered that the number of low-level stratus or stratocumulus clouds are expected to decrease as the planet continues to warm. One **study**, in the journal Nature Climate Change, used satellite observations to discover how cloud formation is affected by ocean temperatures, wind speed, humidity and other factors — and then analysed how those factors will change as the world warms.*

*"We concluded that as the ocean warms, the low-level clouds over the oceans tend to dissipate," said Myers, one of the authors of the study. That means that there are fewer clouds to reflect sunlight and cool the earth — and the change in low-level clouds will **also amplify global warming**.*

...

The new cloud research indicates that the lower estimates for warming are highly unlikely. Instead, the recent papers estimate that CO2 levels of 560 ppm would probably result in at least 3 or 3.5 degrees of warming.

That doesn't mean that the world will definitely hit 3 degrees of warming — if countries continue to shift to clean energy, CO2 in the atmosphere could be stabilized at a level significantly below 560 ppm. But it does mean that the most optimistic estimates for how warming will unfold have been taken off the table.

Basically, nearly everything in this article, apart from one claim that some clouds reduce the warming, are completely wrong. After all, their final conclusion (in the last two paragraphs) is that everything is because of the CO2. As I said, scientists have no clue how huge role forests (deforestation in this case) play in Climate Change.

JURIS BOGDANOVS

The levels of Deforestation

In the next images you can see two squares. Each of these squares represents the whole surface of the world. Namely, they visually represent the different volumes of water versus land, and then forests versus the rest of the land. The first image shows how large areas of all land were covered by forests some 400 years ago.

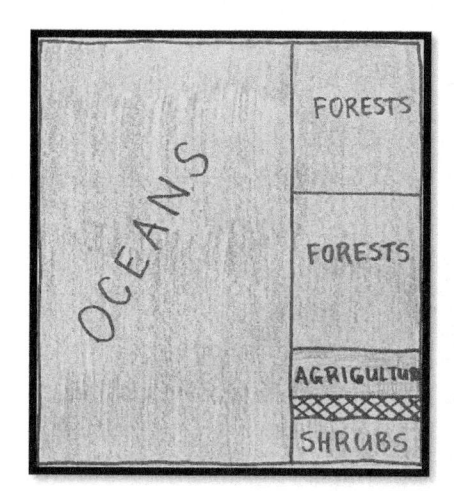

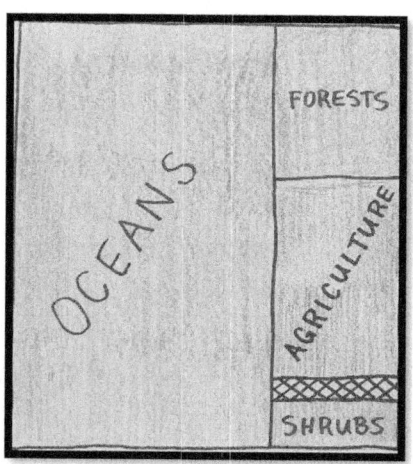

The second image shows how big proportion of all land is left for forests now. And keep in mind that a large portion of these forests are only recovering woodlands. It will take many, many decades for them to recover to their former potential in terms of the mass of their levels and produced humidity around them.

So, at this point I was wondering - What is the current speed of Deforestation, knowing that we are already in crisis with how much forests are left?

https://www.theworldcounts.com/challenges/planet-earth/forests-and-deserts/rate-of-deforestation

Earth's forests are being cut down. And they are being cut down fast

Every year from 2011-2015 about 20 million hectares of forest was cut down. Then things started to speed up. Since 2016, an average of 28 million hectares have been cut down every year. **That's one football field of forest lost every single second around the clock.**

Well, most people aren't even scared of these numbers as they really don't understand them because of the scale of those numbers. Some people even think that the size of the football field isn't that big at all. But that is a lost FOREVER forest, and this area is lost every single second, no exceptions, and no brakes from that process... In total, however, the world is losing around 280 thousand square kilometres annually. Some small countries in Europe, like Latvia, are only 65 thousand square kilometres large in total... So, every year the world loses woodlands that are similar to 4 areas of Latvia.

Area of the **United Kingdom** is around **240 thousand square kilometres**, but the world loses 280 each year. Italy (with around 300 thousand square kilometres) is only slightly larger than this annually lost area of forests. And nobody, not a single scientist is panicking, let alone politicians. Instead, they keep kicking the CO2 levels for no reason at all. There is an old English saying that perfectly fits into this situation – **who needs enemies if we have leaders and scientists like these**...

https://ourworldindata.org/forest-area

How much of the Earth's surface is forested?

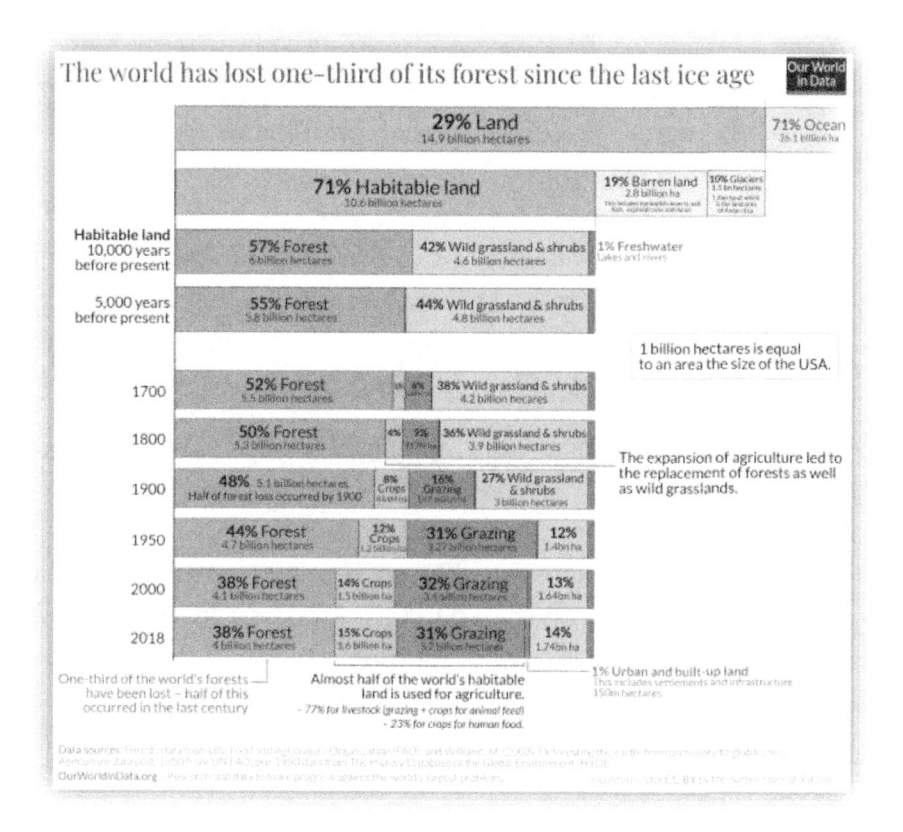

I presented to you this image because it provides different data from what I said previously. Here it says that the world has lost around one third of woodlands it used to have. My claim about 45 to 50% came from other sources, and it was even said so on Wikipedia some time ago. Right now they too have changed it. Yet, in Wikipedia it is said that the world currently has only **31%** of its landmass covered by woods instead of **37%** as in the previous article... If those 31% are correct, then it would be closer to **45 to 50%** lost woodlands from what the Earth used to have thousands of years ago.

Wikipedia:

> ***Deforestation*** *or **forest clearance** is the removal of a **forest** or stand of trees from land that is then **converted** to non-forest use. Deforestation can involve conversion of forest land to **farms**, **ranches**, or **urban** use. The most concentrated deforestation occurs in **tropical rainforests**. About <u>**31% of Earth's land surface** is covered by forests at present</u>. This is one-third less than the **forest cover** before the expansion of agriculture, with half of that loss occurring <u>in the last century</u>. Between 15 million to 18 million **hectares** of forest, an area the size of **Bangladesh**, are destroyed every year. On average <u>2,400 trees are cut down each minute</u>.*

Well, this must be a very old info, as Bangladesh is "only" 148 thousands of square kilometres large. As we already learned from other sources, the current rate of deforestation is around 280 thousands of square kilometres. Yes, there are lots of misinformation going around when it comes to deforestation. Also, if the world used to have **57%** covered by woods, and now there are only **31%** left, then it is much more than one third of lost woodlands, and underreporting isn't even addressed here...

JURIS BOGDANOVS

How to calculate the loss of water in the atmosphere due to deforestation

Now remember the quote where science said that a fully grown tree has around 20 thousand leaves and in one season sprays back into atmosphere around 40 tons of water? Let's do a bit of calculations here. If the world is losing 2'400 trees every minute, and those are trees that are lost forever, then we can easily calculate how much water atmosphere is losing because of these lost trees. So, in one year there are **60x24x365 = 525'600** minutes. This number multiplied by those 2'400 lost trees per minute leads to a total annual loss of **1.26 million of them**. If we multiply this with 40 tons of water..., then we get the staggering **50.4 billion (!!!) tons** of water that atmosphere is not receiving annually. Actually, the atmosphere loses this amount of water every year in some kind of arithmetical progression. Namely, in the year when we start to calculate it, the atmosphere would lose those **50.4 billion tons of water**. The next year it would be another 50.4 on top of that. The next year it would be another 50.4 still on top of the previous year and so on...

So, I was wondering how much are these **50 billion tons** of water in terms of comprehensible volume? Turns out it is around **50 thousand square kilometres, as 1 litre is the same as 1 kilogram**... This is a volume area that would make a pool which is **100 kilometres by 100 kilometres large, and it would be 5 kilometres deep**. I bet no scientist has ever told you this... And this is the volume of water our atmosphere is not receiving every year on top of those waters that it has lost in all previous centuries together.

You could be able to comprehend this volume better if we compared it with an actual water basin. And on this occasion I would like to compare it with the lake **Baikal** in Russia.

Wikipedia:

> With **23,615.39 km³** (5,670 cu mi) of water, Lake Baikal is the world's **largest freshwater** lake by volume, containing **22–23% of the world's fresh surface water.**

Well, as you can see, the volume of the lake Baikal appears to be half the size of what the atmosphere loses every year additionally because of additionally lost woodlands. No wonder rivers and lakes are drying up, and glaciers and polar caps are shrinking. We will talk about them a bit later too.

Yes, these numbers are mind-blowing. And yet, they all come from what the science itself has provided to us but has failed to see how they are linked with Climate Change. Also, we have to keep in mind that not all of this water would stay in the air at the same time, as it would be coming down frequently if there is more vapour entering the air. After all, those 50 thousand square kilometres of water are annual turnover of water cycles.

Now, let us calculate how much water in total the Atmosphere is not receiving because the world has lost those 20 million sq. km. of forests. So, if we had that calculation about the lost moisture from currently disappearing forests of 280 thousand sq. km, and we compared it with 20 million sq.km lost in total, then the world has been losing around **71 times more water annually**. Also, as I said, we have to keep in mind that many of the existing forests are only recovering ones and deforestation is heavily underreported too. So, for that reason, I think it is safe to round up and assume that the world has lost 100 times the volume of those 50 billion tons of water. This would add up to 5000 billion tons of water. And if that is the case, it is very easy to calculate how much water we our atmosphere is not receiving annually due to Deforestation. And that would make a square that is **1000 kilometres by 1000 kilometres with the same**

depth of 5 km as previously. The surface area of this "pool" would be **1 million sq. km.**, and that is the area of **Egypt**.

If we divide these **5000 billion tons** of water by **360 days**, then we arrive at the current daily loss of water in atmosphere. And that would be **137 million tons**. This, in my view, perfectly explains the lower Relative Humidity, all draughts and temperature changes, floods etc...

This amount isn't that big, actually. Turns out, world's population's daily consumption is **10 billion tons** of water, according to **www.theworldcounts.com**. If these numbers are correct, then it is **73 times more** than the atmosphere doesn't receive daily. At this point it is important that the reader understands at least 2 things. First, humidity and precipitation is created by the water vapor and remaining forests too. That means, there is way more water in the air at any given time than those 137 tons. Secondly, we know that we are overusing world's drinking waters and, therefore, we are running out of them.

As said previously, higher temperatures lead to higher total amount of water in air. And that creates many unwanted paradoxes. First of all, there are larger temperature swings because of lower Relative Humidity. This problem leads to air being able to heat up more, as it is dryer, and with increasing temperatures the total amount of water in air also increases. But higher temperatures end up with faster and more significant drop of them when the source of heat goes. In this case, huge amounts of water are forced to fall over very short periods, leading to larger and more frequent floods compared to what they used to be.

At the same time compared to similar temperatures in the past, the air contains less water. And dryer air is more fire-friendly. And nothing changes with higher total humidity because of increase of temperatures, as higher temperatures allow the fire to work even if the humidity is higher too. So, even if the total humidity is higher than it used to be hundreds of years ago, higher temperatures allow the burning process to succeed. It is well known that for the fire to work successfully there is a need of higher temperatures and lower humidity. Cold and moist air supresses fires/wildfires. But when the fire has started, then high moisture alone cannot stop it. This is why we have more frequent and larger wildfires all over the world, many of which remain underreported, like those that take place in Russia.

So, as I said, lower Relative Humidity at given temperatures lead to higher chances of wildfires. And this is exactly what we are observing. Also, knowing that deforestation is moving on at incredible speeds, we can predict that it is only going to become worse. I have never seen so many cracks in soil all over the place where I live right now. I see those cracks increasing from year to year, even in spring time, when it is supposed to be fairly wet all around us. The land keeps creating cracks because it is too dry. And you know what? Cracks lead to faster drying out of the soil as they open the soil up for drying process... Why is it drying out? Because the air itself is dryer. And dry air is attracting water. Yes, the water doesn't simply fly up by itself. It is the molecules of air, most likely the famous Oxygen, who picks up tiny droplets of water and takes them up. So, when the cracks appear, the air starts to pull out the water from the walls of it. This is known as drying process. The air is unable to do that only in situations when it is already saturated with water. But, as we know it, the air is drying up right now... And the only force that can bring back that higher humidity and stop soil from drying up is the increase of the total green mass of plants all around the world.

The next problems that arise from this lower Relative Humidity are greater periods of draughts followed by stronger rainfalls. Of course, I already mentioned the reasons for these heavier rainfalls. However, there is another thing that contributes to devastation because of floods that are caused by the low Relative Humidity. It is known as the **Sponge Effect**! What happens with sponges, effectively, is that dry sponges do not absorb water. If you put a dry sponge under the flawing water from the tap, the water will simply hit the surface of it and move across and down to the sink. It would take time for the sponge to become wet and start to absorb the water.

Interestingly, when the sponge is wet and already fairly saturated with water, it can absorb incredible volume of water. The water from the tap appears to be disappearing inside of it. It even seems that there was never that much space for the water in it to start with. And this effect, very likely, in the same way works on the land too. So, if currently we have been experiencing increasing periods of draughts and dryer air for years now, which is followed by unexpectedly large rainfalls in one go, then the water is more likely to run over the surfaces and create large and destructive masses of water sweeping everything in their way. And all of that would be because of changed Relative Humidity that itself is a consequence of Deforestation.

And even that isn't the whole list of problems created by deforestation. You should remember when in this very book I quoted science which says that the oceans are heating up slower than landmass. And that leads to a very specific problem. As you already know, at lower temperatures the air can keep less water in it. So, since the air above the land is hotter, it can keep a larger amount of water up there. But when this air moves above the ocean, it instantly starts to cool. But lower temperatures cause rain in the air that has too high humidity for these new conditions, which leads to rainfall above the sea. And the air that come from much warmer areas does indeed have higher humidity. In essence, the existing conditions (when the air above the waters is cooler because there is an increasing difference between the temperatures of waters and land) lead to more rainfall above the oceans, which doesn't help us at all.

Of course, there has always been a difference between the temperatures above the land compared to temperatures above the waters. But now these differences are increasing, and that affects some things in water cycles too.

Another thing that might be a side effect of lower Relative Humidity (caused by deforestation) is the increased strength of Sunrays, or, in other words, the atmosphere is less able to supress the impact of Sunrays compared to how it was centuries ago. And that could be a contributing factor in the increase of skin cancer cases too. But at this stage it is a mere speculation. One thing is interesting though to mention with respect to this claim – in one of his science documentaries <u>Professor Brian Cox said this:</u> "**The sun is gradually becoming brighter, and we don't know why...**". But if you think about it, and water indeed resists the electromagnetic energy of Sun, then this lower Relative Humidity once again could be a big part in these processes. Namely, the Sun might not be becoming brighter/stronger, we simply might be experiencing it as brighter and stronger because one of the elements in atmosphere, the one that has been protecting us from it, has been significantly reduced...

JURIS BOGDANOVS

WE ARE KILLING THE PLANET THROUGH DEFORESTATION!

Now, based on these numbers of deforestation (<u>280 thousand square kilometres each year</u>), try to calculate how many years it will take to level the remaining forests at the existing speed of deforestation. So, if **ON THE PAPER TODAY** we have around **40 million square kilometres of forests**, than at the current speed of deforestation it would take only around 140 year to erase the remaining ones. In reality, it will be much faster for various reasons. First of all, as I said it previously, too many areas that are described as forests today (on the paper) are recovering woodlands which have been cut down and now are slowly growing back. We have no idea how large this underreported area is. But that means - these areas have no wood that could be used for anything. And it will take many decades before they reach at least certain maturity. Secondly, the numbers of populations are growing, and so is their prosperity. But that means – demand for goods, including wood, keeps growing...

If we put all of this together, and the numbers of population are growing, and so is their prosperity (read- demand for goods) it wouldn't surprise me that we only have some 60 to 70 years before all forests of this world are gone. But we are in terrible situation already... Deforestation has already led to disrupted water cycles and dryer, warmer climate. The drying out of soil in many regions around the world, including those regions where crops are being grown, has reached the border beyond which those places might turn into deserts. Once we will be there, it is nearly impossible to bring them back, as it leads to a total soil erosion. Look how many deserts China has created with its deforestation decades ago. Even if we will manage to afforest some of them back, it will take thousands of years before those lands become useful for growing crops again. And if you think that China now is leading by example because it plants more forests than it cuts (at least on the paper), think again. The thing is - this statement about the great afforestation in China is true when we talk about territories within China itself. However, China satisfies its never-ending-to-grow demand for woods by cutting down Russia's woodlands. But Russia's woodlands are as important for the climate as are Amazone's Rainforests. The ecosystems don't have borders...

The world is completely connected when it comes to water cycles and humidity. A climate disaster in one country easily leads to consequences in all others too. Destroying Russia's and Brazil's forests will come at a huge cost to the whole world (including China itself) and the "pay-day" might be few years from now. **Today is 6th of June of 2023**...

To understand this better, you all should watch the documentary called – **Pumped Dry**. If you haven't watched this documentary, trust me, you know absolutely nothing about the Climate Change. The message of this documentary is eye-opening and terrifying... And no scientist is addressing this with the due seriousness. Instead, they are kicking the CO2 emissions and many of them are even in denial of human made Climate Change altogether. <u>Who needs enemies</u>..., right?!

In that documentary that I just mentioned (Pumped Dry), it is explained how the world is gradually losing groundwater which is being used t irrigate the crop fields. That water is rapidly diminishing, and huge areas of arable land will inevitably be lost. So, what do we do to save our planet and even ourselves, our kids from death caused by starvation that will be a result of collapse of water cycles followed by the collapse of most ecosystems, crop yields and even of life itself as we know it on Earth today? Nothing! We pretend to fight Climate Change by hating CO2 levels that have no role in all of these problems to start with... **Who needs enemies indeed**...

Before we move on to the problem of overpopulation, which so many seemingly intelligent people are in denial about, and which is the leading force of Deforestation, we have to look at the problem of glaciers, mountain tops, and polar caps. And we have to figure out how this lower Relative Humidity (caused by Deforestation) is responsible for them too.

The problem with the glaciers, mountain tops, and polar caps.

Famously, the volume of ice at these places is diminishing. And once again, the CO2 levels are being blamed. I hope that even the most dedicated haters of the CO2 levels are presently already considering other factors and are ready to do their own research on Deforestation. Clearly, Deforestation is to blame for shrinking glaciers and polar caps too. And yes, it all starts with the same good, old Relative Humidity...

We are told that glaciers and polar caps are melting because of higher temperatures on Earth. And, partly, it is true. At least it can be described as true. However, to understand what is really going on we should understand all aspects leading to it and, especially, start by understanding the formation of these ice layers. So tell me, do you know how they form?

It is actually very easy to understand these processes. In order to do that, think about the freezer in your fridge. You know that the ice layers keep growing in there and we have to defrost them frequently to get rid of all those ice walls. So, where does all that ice come from if there are no precipitation inside the fridge, right?!

Turns out it is a very simple process. In this process the humidity of the air is the one that delivers water to these freezing walls and then it gets frozen there. In essence, the bounds between ice crystals created from water by low temperatures are stronger than bonds between water and oxygen or other gasses. So, whenever a tiny bit of water from air touches a freezing surface, it sticks to it. In this way the layers of ice keep growing. And glaciers, polar caps are growing in exactly the same way. But that means – the level of humidity in air might be very important in regrowing of the ice in these places as no ice will come from a dry air.

I remember the teacher in one of science classes (in 80-ies, in Soviet Union) telling us that the mount Kilimanjaro in Africa has lost its ice cap in summers. And he said that it has started in some 70-ties, if I am correct. Before that it was known to locals (and everyone else) for its top being covered by ice eternally. He said that it was even called "the eternally white top", or something like that. Already then the teacher said that it is a consequence of human activities, and that this is because the world is heating up because of us.

I believe that after everything that has been addressed in this book it is a no-brainer to realise that changes in humidity might be central to this problem too. Think of it! A higher humidity not only reduces the temperatures that reach the surface of Earth, but also provides more material for building up the ice mass of glaciers, mountain tops, or polar caps. Yes, they are growing from the top, from the moisture in the air. After all, there are mountains that are above the clouds. And they are all covered with ice.

Now, since the Relative Humidity is diminishing, it is only logical to conclude that ice is simply not returning to those places at the same speed as it used to. Also, since less water in air leads to higher temperatures, then even increased total humidity because of higher total temperatures doesn't help as for the freezing to be possible there is a need of slightly lower temperatures. So, even if the temperatures have risen only a tiny amount, it still is enough to influence the growing back of the ice because the periods of when the ice is melting have increased in terms of time and intensity. Clearly, this reduction of ice takes place at a very slow rate, as those are small changes after all. That is true especially if we look at these facts from the perspective of one year period. However, when this is now happening and getting worse every single year, the speed of loss of ice mass is increasing too... And the melting ice cap of mount Kilimanjaro didn't start in 70-ties or 80-ties. It only become visible at a certain point.

Let's remember that in 70-ties there were already 4 billion people in the world and deforestation levels have been moving towards their peak for two hundred years already.

I remember my own childhood in Latvia (then under Soviet Union) in 80-ies. All winters were just filled with large masses of snow, which we enormously enjoyed as kids. We had at least 3 months of fairly thick and permanently present snow all around us. Later, in 90-ties, the snow seemed to have vanished. Of course, I moved to live and learn in a region that is located at lower altitudes too. But I frequently visited those previous places and there was less snow there too. Also, people in the new location also kept saying that they used to have much more snow. It was like the snow was simply cut off from our reality. Yes, there still was some on some years, but it was nothing like it used to be. And the one thing that I realised later was that it wasn't snowing that much anymore. That seemed especially obvious compared with the time in 80-ties. There was so much less precipitation. Even if the temperatures were slightly higher on average, the weather still was cold enough for the snow to stay if it came. But it didn't. So, that for me explained it all – there was less precipitation... I didn't have any interest in exploring the levels of humidity in those days, but things have clearly been changing...

Not so long ago I was listening to a discussion on the **radio LBC**. It was about the critical fresh water shortages in the UK. And even though one of the reasons mentioned for that was the fact that the state for decades hasn't been investing in new and additional water reservoirs where to collect it (and population has kept significantly growing thanks to open-door to immigration policies), the people who worked in this system also clearly stated this – there has been significantly less precipitation too. And that is happening in the UK. This country is an island surrounded by seas. Yet, there isn't enough rain to fill the tanks of drinking water. Of course, we know that

Relative Humidity is going down also above the seas. And faster growing temperatures above the land make the raining more likely above the seas, as I explained it previously.

Deforestation visualized

In order to move on with this problem I would like to share with you some facts about the drying up Colorado River in the USA, about diminishing glaciers of that region and history of deforestation. This is another great example of how deforestation has affected humidity and precipitation and, therefore, the water levels in our rivers and lakes. So, this is the story of the **Colorado River**. It is losing water rapidly year after year, as do many rivers in China and others around the world. Colorado river starts in mountains of **state Colorado**, location of which you can see in this image.

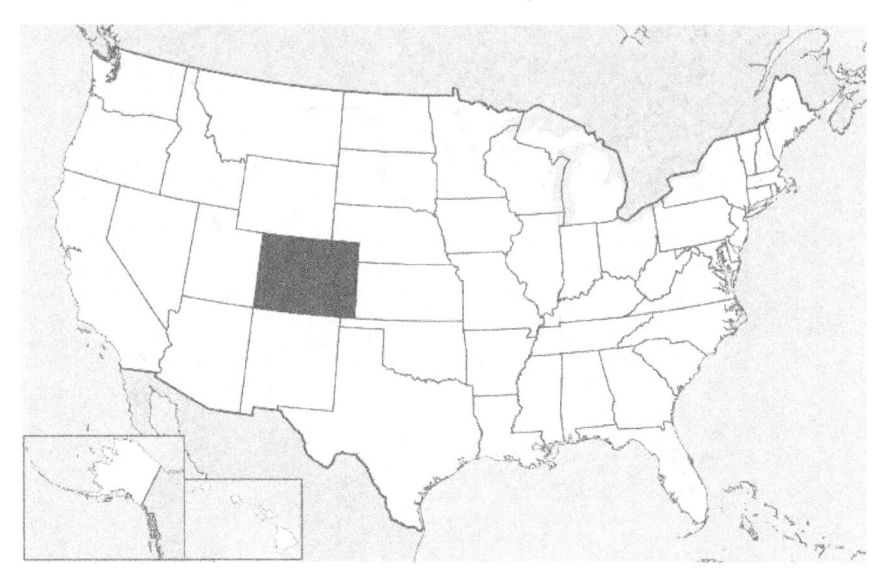

The Colorado river is incredibly long and moves in both directions from the Colorado mountains. It used to be the area that was richly covered by what the science calls – **the Virgin Forests**. Those are large woodlands that consist of old and huge trees. They have nearly vanished due to deforestation, as can be seen in next images.

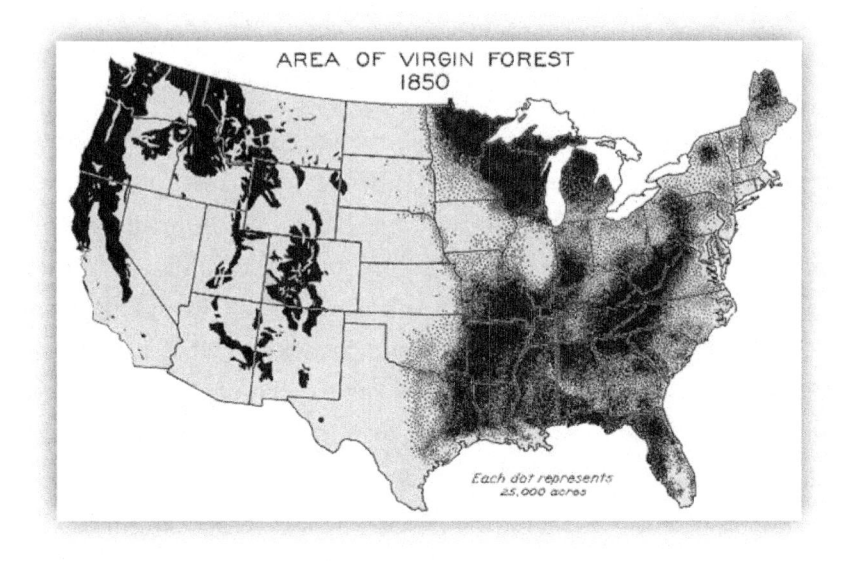

AREA OF VIRGIN FOREST 1850

AREA OF VIRGIN FOREST 1926

These images show the total number of **lost Virgin Forests in the USA** over a period of some **180 years**. It doesn't include territories that are being cleared currently. Maybe they stopped it, as there is nearly nothing left of them anyway, as you can see. In essence, the darker areas in these images represent territories that used to be covered by these Virgin Forests. America has really cleared them. And look at the state Colorado itself. Of course, there were huge woodlands on the east and north-west of the USA too. It is hard to tell but it looks that they could have lost around 95% of their Virgin Forests.

These forests produced the humidity in a larger area around Colorado. That moisture deposited also on **<u>Colorado mountains forming large ice caps and glaciers</u>** there. In summers, when there were less rain, these glaciers were melting providing Colorado River with extra water. In this way the river was kept full all the time. Now it has changed. Some estimates say that it is half deep as it used to be. Of course, a lot of water is used in irrigation. Yet, it didn't start yesterday. But the levels of water in it keep dropping. It might dry out one day.

Nature does indeed work in surprising ways. But since the forests have vanished in huge volumes, it has led to less precipitation in large areas, and the ice caps of mountains and glaciers cannot regenerate themselves because of lower Relative Humidity and slightly higher temperatures. The melting of the glaciers in summers might be happening at the same or similar pace as it used to, but there is simply less and less material to be melted. Their ice mass isn't regrowing as it used too when the forests were there. And similar picture can be seen nearly everywhere in the world – the less woodlands we have, the lower the levels of water in lakes and rivers, and the less ice on glaciers and mountain tops. It is especially informative when we look at what is happening in China.

The world will run out of drinking water because of Deforestation

theguardian.com, (22. August, 2022...)

> *China drought causes Yangtze to dry up, sparking shortage of hydropower.*
>
> *A record-breaking drought has caused some rivers in **China** – including parts of the Yangtze – to dry up, affecting hydropower, halting shipping, and forcing major companies to suspend operations.*
>
> *A nationwide drought alert was issued on Friday as **a long-running and severe heatwave** in China's heavily populated south-west was forecast to continue well into September.*
>
> *The loss of water flow to China's extensive hydropower system has sparked a "grave situation" in Sichuan, which gets more than 80% of its energy from hydropower.*

Yes, China has experienced never before seen drought. As you know, China's forests are increasing instead of decreasing. But that started only after they realised what they have done with huge deforestation levels. Still, why the droughts are hitting them now, right? As I already said, China is cutting Russia's forests. And the closer to their borders, the better, because transportation costs too. But ecosystems, especially the large ones, are globally connected. So, the disappearing forests in Russia lead to increase of draughts, first of all, in warmer places close to it. And China is right below Russia towards the equator.

Virgin Forests are important because they consist of very old and tall trees. These trees have the largest mass of wood (CO2 depositories) and the largest mass of green leaves which are the tools for creating oxygen and humidity in the atmosphere. Sometimes the size matters. And we have lost enormous amounts of these things. And stopping Deforestation, let alone starting Afforestation, isn't an option yet for humankind. I don't know why!

https://ourworldindata.org

> *Global deforestation reached its peak in the 1980s. We lost 150 million hectares – an area half the size of India – during that decade. Clearing of the Brazilian Amazon for pasture and croplands was a major driver of this loss.*
>
> *Since then, deforestation rates have steadily declined, to 78 million hectares in the 1990s; 52 million in the early 2000s; and 47 million in the last decade.*

As I said, the existing mechanisms combined with lower humidity lead not only to increased droughts, but also to increased floods. We have been observing droughts by now, but at some point terrible floods could hit the country too. All consequences of terrible levels of Deforestation all around the world.

And now we are ready to learn about the problem of population numbers... You must have heard somebody saying, that there are too many people in this world. And there are some others, including the world-famous entrepreneur Elon Musk and quite a few other intellectuals, who think that there is not enough people on Earth, and we should do our best to increase our numbers. So, which of these opinions is correct, right?! To understand that we have to look at the current use of all land once again.

The world will run out of habitable land for agriculture

https://ourworldindata.org/land-use

Half of the world's habitable land is used for agriculture

For much of human history, most of the world's land was wilderness: forests, grasslands and shrubbery dominated its landscapes. Over the last few centuries, this has changed dramatically: wild habitats have been squeezed out by turning it into agricultural land.

If we rewind 1000 years, it is estimated that only 4 million square kilometres – **less than 4% of the world's ice-free and non-barren land area was used for farming**.

Global land use for food production

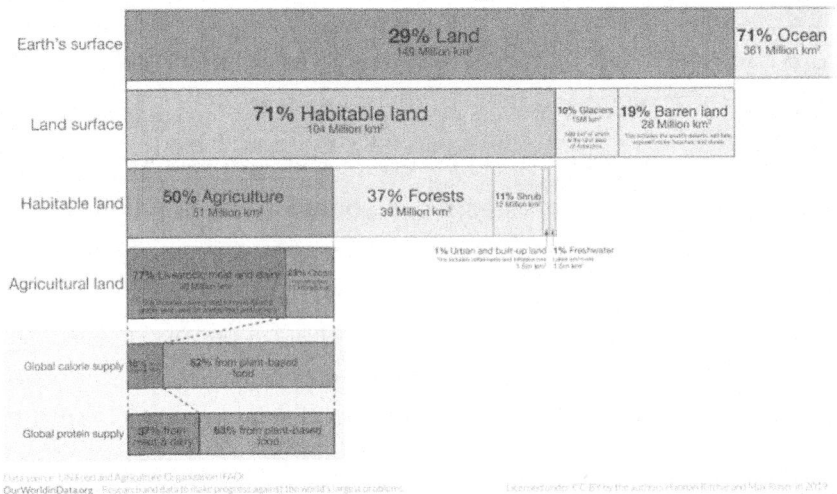

Here is visually described the use of all land the Earth has. As you can see, only **71%** of all land surface is described as habitable... And **50%** of it is already being used for Agriculture – for growing food. It says here that **37% of this Habitable Land are forests**. Well, if we look at the <u>whole land mass, then it could be that forests are only **31%** of it compared to it</u>, as that is stated in other sources.

Well, one thing to keep in mind right now is that we have taken huge areas away from forests. And, to restore a healthy water cycles, we should rebuild them. So, what is important to understand here is that those should be solid Virgin Forests, which we would keep there without cutting them. It will take time! Also, since the need for woodlands will always exist, we should dedicate some areas where we grow and harvest forests for our consumption, and never use more than we can regrow. But, for that to be possible, we have to dedicate large areas of land to forests. **AND THOSE AREAS SHOULD REALLY BE HUGE, AS THE WORLD HAS LOST FORESTS THAT ARE SIMILAR TO TWO CHINAS OR THE WHOLE RUSSIA TOGETHER WITH KAZAKHSTAN.** Compare the size of these areas with the total landmass of the world.

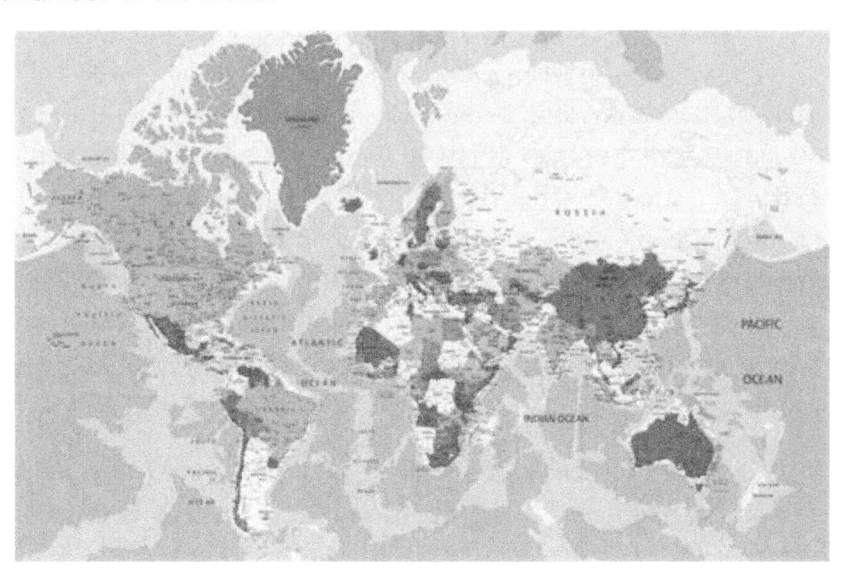

Such a huge loss of forests, obviously, will lead to huge impact on climate. And restoration of these forested areas would lead to a huge reduction of arable land available for Agriculture... So, what do we do and how much we have to sacrifice, where we have to adjust and/or compromise to, right?!

Well, to start with, we will have to change our diet, as production of animal meat takes around **77% (!!!)** of all the land we use for Agriculture. This is confirmed by science as can be seen in the previous chart. But the meat production only secures **18% of all calory supply** globally and **37% of all protein supply** globally.

The previous information means - **We will have to get used to poultry** (birds meat) **alone**, as it needs much less land to produce similar amount of food and nutrients. And we will have to do it as soon as possible. Another thing that should be changed significantly is the population numbers... Very soon you will understand why the rush! TRUST ME, THERE IS NO ESCAPING THIS TASK!

Some sceptics keep claiming that there is no danger, and the numbers of humans could be much higher without endangering the ecosystems of the world. Sometimes they say this - if we put all people of the whole world side to side in one place, so that they each have a **1 square meter** for them, it would only take **8 billion square meters**. One square kilometre has **1 million square meters in it**. One thousand square kilometres would accommodate 1 billion. That means – **8 thousand sq. km** is enough for the whole world. Ireland is 10 times larger than that, as it has **82 thousand sq. km**. A tiny weeny area, right? No reason to worry about the overpopulation... Or is it?

Everything changes when we look at how much land one person needs to provide himself with the food. I used the online calculator to figure it out.

The next information comes from the article: **How Much Land Does It Take To Feed One Person – Online Calculator** (by **William Swanson**)

So, the smallest amount of land need to feed one person is obtained if you only use vegetables, fruit, and storage for all that food. Basically, you are **a vegan-hardliner**. In this case it is said that you will only need around <u>**0.38 hectares** to feed yourself for one year</u>.

The largest amount of land is needed if **you eat everything**. Namely, you eat all kinds of meat and stop at nothing. In this case one person will need around **4 hectares** per person to feed himself. I used this information to multiply 8 billion humans by those "**vegan 0.38 hectares**". It gave me around **3 billion hectares** of land. Since there are 100 hectares in one square kilometre, then I divided these 3 billion by 100 and now we have **30 million km²**. Yes, this is the smallest amount of land needed to properly feed 8 billion people, who all would have to be vegans. Right now the world is using around 52 million sq. km (50% of all habitable land) for Agriculture. And to save the planet, we should return to nature those 20 million square kilometres... So, we would be left with 32 million sq. km of land for food... This is the first clear indication that there are too many people in this world.

Since Europe, China and USA are close to **10 million km²** each, then the territories of all three of them taken together would represent the area of land available to us to provide the existing population of the world with the most basic demand for food. At this point it would be right for you to keep in mind that only around 43% of China is actually habitable land... And there are huge deserts and mountain ranges in the USA too which cannot be used for agriculture. The same, on a much smaller scale though, goes for Europe. That means, we will need much more of the worlds land to feed the 8 billion large population.

If all these **8 billion humans** wanted a maximum comfort in terms of food supplies, and that means 4 hectares would be needed to provide the food for each of them, then the total land needed for Agriculture should be more than **10 times (!!!)** larger than those **30 million km²**.

Namely, we would need around **320 million km²** of arable land dedicated to Agriculture, in order to provide ourselves with food. But total dry land of Earth is only around **150 million km²**... And only **70%** (**105 million km²**) of it is habitable... and **50%** (**52.2 million km²**) of it is already dedicated to Agriculture... And 37% of the habitable land are covered with forests, but that must increase at least twice...

Just ponder for a while over these numbers... Think especially hard about the fact that we should afforest back, possibly, at least some **20 million km²** of land and started to do it immediately. But since we already use **50 million km²** of all habitable land for Agriculture, and since the minimum needed to properly feed <u>**8 billion** humans</u> is **30 million km²**, and we cannot afford anymore to cut down forests, then we have to admit that by replanting those forests we definitely have reached the border of land use and our numbers beyond which the destruction of the planet will be irreversible.

And we can only save the planet if we abandon absolutely everything, and all 8 billion people started to plant forests like crazy. And even in this case it would only help if the currently remaining **40 million km²** of forests actually were Virgin Forests and absolutely everybody on Earth was vegan, which is not the case and, most likely, never will be. So, if we have those **30 million sq. km.** for food, and we all eat everything we want to, then this world can only provide with food around **750 million people**. This is the number that we had right <u>before the Industrial Revolution</u>... Clearly, today we are way over this number... In fact, we are **10.6 times** over this number. But some countries are 50 and even 100 times above this HEALTHY FOR THE PLANET NUMBER OF POPULATION.

It might help if I told you currently each human, from those 8 billion on this planet currently, has only **1.3 hectares (3.2 acres)** of habitable land, if we divided all the **105 million sq. km** of habitable land by those 8 billion. And one third of it are still forests. Another one third should be afforested back. And that leaves us with 40% of these 1.3 hectares for where to grow food. So, these 40% of 1.3 are **0.5 hectares (1.2 acres)**. At this moment it is good to remember what you learned just few paragraphs before. Namely, we have run out of land for the current population of the world because we need more land for food than we have. And this, in my view, perfectly explains why there are too many people on this world.

With this in mind it is interesting to watch discussions in the USA, where Conservative party is trying to abolish abortions. Not only that takes away a huge proportion of votes in elections from them, as at least 90% of all women feel very strongly for this right, but that also will lead to increase of population numbers there. **USA** only has **87 people** per square kilometre. With this density applied to the whole world, there would be around **9 million** people, but that is around **10 to 12 times too high** density already. And we all know that USA is already drying out.

America's density seems not so big compared to China's 147, let alone India's 400 plus, or South Korea's 500 plus, but it still is way above what should be considered too much. On top of that, the US is said to be using only around 53% of its land, and 47% are uninhabited. But that means, the density of population on these 53% of inhabited land is **164 people per sq. km**. If we applied this density to the habitable land of the world, we would get **17 billion** people on Earth today with the existing density of the USA. So, as you can see, there is absolutely nothing to celebrate about these numbers, and the density of the USA is at least 22 times too high. And we are doing absolutely nothing to fix this problem of Deforestation! Remember and always keep in mind that we currently are cutting down around **280 thousand sq. km** of forests annually, and those that we cut but let grow back aren't even included in this number. In fact, we don't even know it, even though it is extremely important to understand the whole scale of the damage. And this permanently lost territory, as I said, is slightly larger than the whole United Kingdom.

All of that means - we are dragging the Earth towards a total destruction. After all, Deforestation keeps increasing and numbers of humans keep doubling every 50 years or so... And this is why I don't understand those people who keep saying that this world is somehow still ok, let alone that we need much more people here.

One of the most bizarre experiences of mine, with respect to this problem, was listening to rants of **Radio LBC** presenters, who just kept pedalling this idea about Earth needing more humans, including England. Have they ever seen the numbers? Also, they were prising India's rapidly raising population numbers and laughing about Chinas stagnating ones. How did we get here where illiterate and ignorant people are in charge of information, politics and even science??? And they even manage to sell themselves as the most literate and smart guys of all... The world is really in a very sad place right now. In essence, we are sleepwalking into self-destruction, and we fight demons that aren't real and have been made-up by our wishful thinking. CO2 as a problem is one of these made-up demons... And nobody is scared. They will be, in few years' time, when the global starvation will kick in. But then it will be too late. Then we will pay a full price and the hard way.

And the actual reality is even grimmer...

Wikipedia:

> *According to the* **Food and Agriculture Organization** *of the United Nations, in 2013, the world's arable land amounted to* **1.407 billion hectares**, *out of a total of 4.924 billion hectares of land used for agriculture...*

1.4 billion hectares are the same as **14 million km²**. Russia is **17 million km²** large. And these **14 million km²** are specifically dedicated to growing crops and other plant food. But there are also grazing lands for animals. I already said that we need **30 million square kilometres** to provide the existing population with the most basic amount of plant food if we stop meat consumption. I also said that in total for food production we are currently using around **50% of all habitable land**, which is close to **50 million square kilometres**. And this article of Wikipedia confirms that, as it states that the world is using *4.924 billion hectares (49 million sq. km) of land used for agriculture.* <u>So, what is grimmer about that, right?</u> Let us think about the fact that it appears as if we are currently eating all kinds of food, and somehow we aren't in need of all those **320 million sq. km** at all, as those calculations of mine for the land needed to feed ourselves predicted. So, what is going on?

Turns out, this seeming discrepancy is only possible because only a small part of humankind are provided with full spectrum of food, while the most of humans are living on a very limited amount of it. In fact, starvation is a large part of many societies all around the world, including in the so-called rich countries. After all, those **50 million square kilometres**, if every person was eating everything that is possible, would only provide food for **1.25 billion people**. Reminder – it would be 750 million with 30 million sq. km, which is top area we can afford to dedicate to Agriculture without damaging water cycles on Earth.

Of course, I also said that 30 **million km²** would provide **8 billion** people, if absolutely everyone became a vegan. But let's face it – it isn't going to happen as most people chose to eat the whole spectrum of foods no matter what. Secondly, these **8 billion** still would need wooden products, water for different needs etc. Also, majority of people in the world today aren't big consumers of wood for the same reason for which they aren't consuming meat – they are extremely poor. And the larger number of people become prosperous, the higher becomes their consumption rates of all types of things... And the world leaders are doing their best, at least they say they are doing their best; to increase prosperity of everyone all over the world and they are striving to increase the numbers of population too. Good luck with that!

When talking about the current food supply, we also have to admit that some countries have achieved incredible efficiency in food production, especially in countries like the Netherlands. This is a very small country, but at the same time it is the second largest food importer in the world right after the USA. Unfortunately, while this topic on its own could make an interesting story, we aren't addressing it in this book. One thing is important to mention though – some globalists and CO2 haters are doing their absolutely best to reduce the food production in quite a few countries. And only one of them is Netherlands. Among others are countries like Ireland, Canada, New Zealand. Their own governments are forcefully shutting down farms. They are excusing their actions with the need to fight the Climate Change, and their main culprit is, of course, CO2... At this moment it should be clear to any reader that we might be on the verge of starvation, and closing down food production isn't helping anything here. Funny, Canada is ready to be very harsh with cutting down fertilizers, while the problems of deforestation are at least in the second tenth on their list. But who needs enemies, if we have political leaders like that, right?!

I have a message to all of these political leaders – Stop suppressing the food production! This is really a very bad time for that... Become drastic with achieving Afforestation and stopping Deforestation! We don't have a time for any delays!

As I already said it many times, this planet can only provide with full spectrum of foods (if we restore woodlands) some **0.75 billion** people. Of course, we could find more advanced methods to produce food in larger amounts on smaller territories, and we could change our diet too. Still, I don't think that this planet will be able to support more than **1 billion** people and stay healthy. But that is my current estimate. Maybe this planet can only sustain 250 million people...

So, what do we do, right? Do we kill some of us? I hope not! The only way I see this being achieved is by drastically reducing the birth rates. 1 child per family would be just right. We should stick to it at least till the numbers normalize. After that - 2 child policies! And all societies that aren't willing to take part in this, namely, they want to keep breading without borders, should be restrained to their own territories and forced to provide themselves with their own resources. Otherwise they will take over and destroy the whole planet. After all, resources of arable lands are limited.

Yes I know - these are very drastic measures. However, you should keep in mind that the other option is the global starvation, caused by draughts, which themselves are caused by Deforestation, and that will be much more painful and drastic. In fact it will be so terrifying, that this one-child policy will seem to us like a god's sent blessing and the best thing that could have happened.

Now I would like to introduce you to some interesting facts about the density of populations in different countries. It is very telling and interesting indeed. I don't know why scientists aren't talking about it on a daily basis. These numbers will determine the fate of all of us very, very soon. So, the first county in mind is the United Kingdom, as this is the country in which I currently reside. It turned out to be a very interesting story, especially when I compared it to Latvia. But before we get to the actual numbers, let's take a look at some other, but relevant facts about the UK, obtained from the UK's own government page...

https://www.gov.uk/government/statistics/united-kingdom-food-security-report-2s021

Official Statistics

United Kingdom Food Security Report 2021: Theme 2: UK Food Supply Sources

Updated 22 December 2021

...

Key messages

The biggest medium to long term risk to the UK's domestic production comes from climate change and other environmental pressures like soil degradation, water quality and biodiversity. Wheat yields dropped by 40% in 2020 due to heavy rainfall and droughts at bad times in the growing season. Although they have bounced back in 2021, this is an indicator of the effect that increasingly unreliable weather patterns may have on future production.

...

The UK currently produces about 60% of its domestic food consumption by economic value, part of which is exported. This means just under half of the actual food on plates is produced in the UK, including the majority of grains, meat, dairy, and eggs. This figure would be higher without exports. UK supply comprises domestic production excluding exports, plus imported food. The production to supply ratio, important for understanding the UK's self-sufficiency, has remained stable over the last two decades, and for crops that can be commercially grown in the UK has been around 75%

...

In **2020 71% of UK land area was used for agricultural production**, the majority of this being grassland for grazing rather than crops. Not all land is suitable for growing crops, and some is suitable only for specific crops. Land use overall has changed little in the last thirty years, with annual variation between specific crops due to factors such as the weather and prices rather than long-term or systematic variation. Domestic production faces a number of long-term and short-term risks, including soil degradation, drought and flooding, diseases, risks to fuel and fertiliser supplies, and changing labour markets. In the long term, climate change impacts are likely to have a negative effect on the proportion of high-grade arable farmland available in the UK.

...

Diverse international supply sources

Overreliance on one geographical area and dependence on particular supply sources makes food supply more vulnerable, while diversity of sources makes it more resilient. UK consumer preferences and diets include a range of products that cannot be grown in the UK or cannot be grown year-round. Therefore, the UK does not produce everything it eats or eat everything it produces.

In 2020, the UK imported 46% of the food it consumed. Having a diverse range of international sources makes food supply more resilient, as if the production or output of one source is disrupted, other sources can meet demand. No one country provided more than 11% of those imports, a picture which has been stable for some time. By value, £48 billion of food, feed, and drink (FFD) was imported and £21.4 billion was exported.

The overpopulation of the United Kingdom

Famously, we are used to think that the one country that is heavily overpopulated is China. But the reality is very different. China has indeed a fairly big density. However, it is a really large country. interestingly, when China's density is compared to density in England (not the UK), it has way better situation. And the same is true with when it is compared with some other EU countries, let alone other countries in Asia. So, before we take a closer look at numbers, lets discuss the previous quote.

So, what is the takeaway from this article quoted above, right?! First of all, the UK only produces around **60% of food** that it consumes. And some of that is **exported** as it imports **46% of food** it consumes... **71% of total land** area is already dedicated to Agriculture. And that, instantly, indicates that the UK has already less woodlands than it should for the healthy water cycles. Of course, the global Deforestation affects it too. If you asked me, the UK is already over its limit of how much land it can dedicate to Agriculture, as its woodlands are less than are in the world on average.

Wikipedia:

> *Nowadays, about **13% of Britain's land surface** is wooded. The country's supply of timber was severely depleted during the **First** and **Second** World Wars, when imports were difficult, and the forested area bottomed out at under **5% of Britain's land surface in 1919**. That year, the **Forestry Commission** was established to produce a strategic reserve of timber. As of 2020, other European countries average from 1% (Malta) to 66% (Finland) of their area as woodland.*

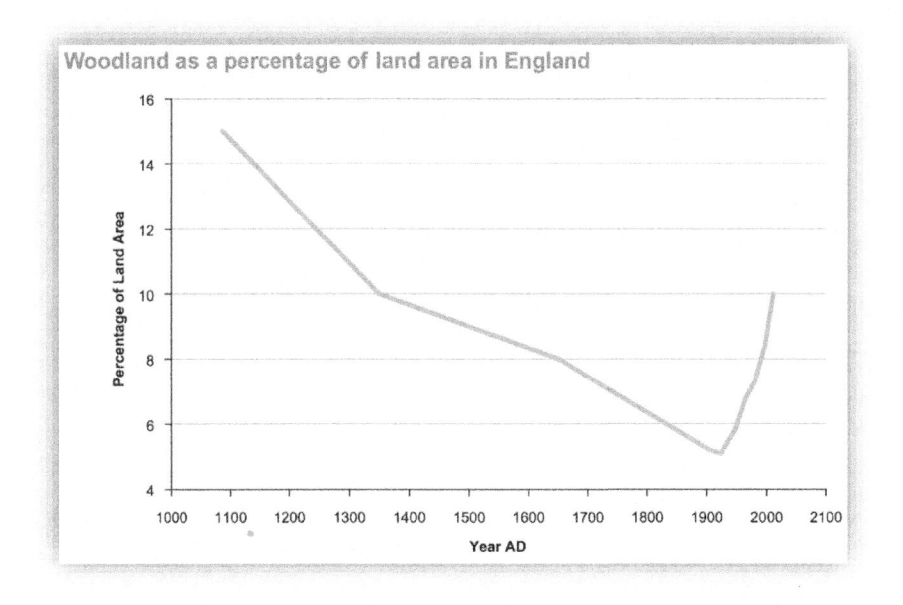

[Chart: Woodland as a percentage of land area in England, showing percentage declining from ~15% in 1000 AD to ~5% around 1900, then rising to ~10% by 2000]

This previous chart shows the coverage of woodlands in Britain for a thousand-year period. It states that Britain never had more than 15% of its land covered by woods, even though this Wikipedia article states that British isles are ideal for the growth of all kinds of trees. And historically here were much less people living. So, why didn't trees overtake the isles? Or are these estimates wrong? I don't know.

Wikipedia:

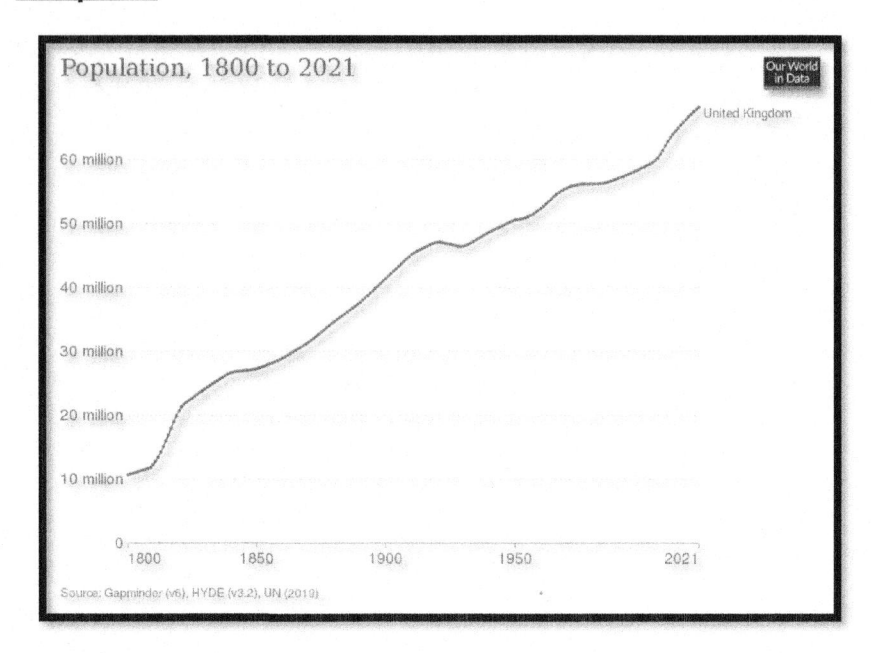

Population, 1800 to 2021 — United Kingdom
(Source: Gapminder (v6), HYDE (v3.2), UN (2019))

As you can see, some 220 years ago there were only 10 million people living in the UK. So, over first 100 years starting from 1800 the numbers increased to 40 million, and then over the next 120 they increased to 67 million. This trend seems to remain steady. And it shows an average increase of population by 25- 30 million over every 100 years. We can safely predict, that if this trend continues, there might be around 80 to 100 million people in the UK by 2100. Let's remember that the UK is only producing 60% of food it consumes already now, and it already uses 70% of all land for Agriculture.

Now, knowing that the world is drying up and the dangers of global starvation are slowly but steadily creeping in, tell me – at what point the population numbers can be considered dangerous if we now that there will be a food crisis in the world? It definitely will come! I would give it a total of 10 years to become clear even to the most intellectually blind person. In fact, I think it will be much sooner. Do you remember how that government article said that in 2020 there was a drop of wheat yield by 40% because of climate change...

So, what the UK is going to do with their open-door policies when it will start? In 2022 alone the immigration has risen by 600 thousand, which is the highest in recorded history. The funny thing is, the UK is outside of the EU, and Brexit happened mainly because of the huge immigration numbers and realisation that there is only as much space in the UK as there is. So, what happened?

The reality is so sad that it is even painful to talk about. Turns out that the so-called **Brexiteers** themselves, including **Boris Johnson**, opened the door for immigration right after the Brexit. What they did is this – they withdraw the caps limiting the numbers of students coming to the UK from India and other countries. That opened the floodgates of immigration. On one hand they reduced immigration from Europe, on the other hand they opened the door to much larger part of the world. Possibly, this was done already by **Teresa May**. Who knows! One thing is clear – Boris Johnson didn't stop it. Now, realising that this is a huge problem, and realising that it will be taken against the Conservative party by voters, the current Prime Minister (**Rishi Sunak**) is actively pretending that he is dealing with immigration very harshly by trying to stop those boat crossings. In fact, they only divert your attention to the minor problem, so that you miss the fact that they are keeping too many doors too open in other places. They are pretending that they are listening to people and acting accordingly, while in reality they do the opposite.

According to UK statistics, in 2022 the number of population increased by 606 thousand due to immigration. But the total number of immigration, according to **the Telegraph**, was 1.2 million. Simply some 500 plus thousand people have left the country.

The Telegraph, 25th May 2023, by Charles Hymas.

UK net migration hits record high despite Tory Pledges

Net migration has hit a record high of 606,000, according to the Office for National Statistics.

The surge has been fuelled by more than **1.2 million migrants, primarily from outside** the EU, being granted visas to enter the UK to study, work or escape conflict or oppression. The ONS estimated that 557,000 people emigrated.

The resulting 606,000 for the year ending December 2022 is nearly **three times the pre-Brexit average of between 200,000 and 250,000**.

If you placed every 3 people of these immigrants into one accommodation unit, you would need 200 thousand new places where to accommodate these 600 thousands. And we know that England is already heavily overpopulated (I will explain that very soon with facts), and that it is heavily short with green areas and forests. So, one would assume that politicians will start to consider limiting the growth of population, if not stopping and starting to reverse them, especially through immigration, right? No! They simply declare that everything will be solved by building more houses for these immigrants as the housing market of the UK is terribly short of them.

And then came ideas of **Labour party**, from **Sir Keir Starmer** himself, that Labour will use green belts for developing new housing projects... Knowing everything we learned in this book, this solution seems like a madman's last trick. Please, read the next quote!

todaysconveyancer.co.uk

Labour will allow more homes to be built on green belt – Keir Starmer

Sir Keir Starmer has said Labor will allow more homes to be on green belt land and relax planning restrictions.

The Labour manifesto states that they would boost homeownership and housebuilding by setting the target of a homeownership rate to 70%. It also states that it would help first-time buyers onto the ladder with a new, comprehensive mortgage guarantee scheme.

Under this scheme, the "state will act as guarantor for prospective homeowners who can afford mortgage repayments but struggle to save for a large deposit".

More on this, the manifesto states that build more high-quality homes across the country and ensure more of these are genuinely affordable and bring the present leasehold system to an end through fundamental reform of the tenure and to enacting legislation to that end as soon as possible.

Dear Sir Starmer! First of all, has it ever occurred to you that simplifying the house purchasing process instantly increases demand for houses in a market that is already severely short on housing? After all, this is exactly why we have these absurd house prices in the UK now. But that means the poor will end up being screwed again. As the saying goes – **the road to hell is paved with good intentions...** And it all starts with a lack of consideration for all aspects of the given question.

We all remember that scheme introduced by Conservative government called **Help2Buy**. It really increased housing prices significantly. Now, on top of that, Central Bank is rising interest rates by several percents, which inevitable will lead to unsustainable payments specifically to those who became part of this Help2Buy. First of all, these people have some of the largest mortgages. Secondly, they are very early in their purchase, which means – their remaining mortgage has the highest value, and they will suffer the most from those interest rates. Together with inflation (all over the place) most of them might lose their houses. So, the whole idea of Help2Buy turns out to be a huge scam. And the suggestion of Labour Party is nothing short of the same thing. Yes, with this initiative you will damage the housing market even further and the poor will take the hardest blow.

So, how exactly are you going to build those houses? Is there an army of builders idly spending their days because there is no house to be built by them? No! The same article also writes this:

> *"We are building less: 2.2 million net additions were built between 1961-71, compared with 1.7m net additions between 2006-2016," the paper says.*
>
> *...*
>
> *Spokesman **Jonathan Rolande** said: ... in the last 13 years "only half of the relatively modest 300,000 requirement have been built due to a combination of planning delays, nimbyism, land-banking, <u>a lack of plentiful skilled labor and shortages of materials</u>."*

As you can see, there are shortages of builders and materials. Where to find them? I have an idea! Why don't we attract some hundreds of thousands more migrants to come and do the job. The problem is, they too will need a housing, schools for their children, places in hospitals for their elderly etc. But with bigger numbers of population also grows the need for police forces, hospital workers, teachers..., let alone hospitals and schools themselves will be needed...

In short, by solving one problem in this way, you create hundreds of others and, actually, even if you built those 200 thousand homes per year, you still would be slagging far behind the demand. So, no problem will be solved in next decade or so. And definitely not if immigration remains as high as it is now. All you will have achieved with this will be larger numbers in everything. Namely, more people in total, larger shortages of nurses and doctors, teachers, policemen, housing, schools and roads and parking places... And all of that in already overpopulated England (as I said, about that you will be informed very soon)... Clearly, that will be followed by even louder cries about the need for more workers, as that will be declared good for economy, as radio LBC and BBC think it will. Yes, the economy will be larger, but so will absolutely all problems of the UK including shortages of workers..., skilled or unskilled, because increase of number of people in one area leads to increase of demand for workers and problems in other ones.

The thing is – the UK, and far too many countries all around the globe, have problems of how the society operates, not how many people there are. The levels of people with obesity and Type 2 diabetes are staggering. There are around 6 million people in the UK alone suffering from this type of diabetes. These people (according to some estimates) take around 50% of the whole NHS budget. Clearly, they take lots of human resources too as these conditions are accompanied by piles of other health issues and very slow healing. No wonder UK is **100 thousand nurses** short. It is unsustainable.

On top of that, and this too isn't typical to the UK alone, there are huge numbers of non-productive jobs and jobs that are more like parasites. The need for extremely large numbers of security personnel is a sign of something terribly wrong in society. More often than not, people working in these areas are very strong, young, and healthy people. They are not available to production. Then there are armies of different layers, entertainers etc. If the money wasted on them was given to manufacturing and production as subsidies, then they could pay very decent salaries and there would never be lack of workers. The same is true with diabetics. They are tired and sick because of their condition. Of course, some of them work too. However, their condition can be altered by a very strict diet, and they would become perfectly fit for any work. Most importantly, they wouldn't take the human and financial resources from the NHS. And our governments have already proved that they can be extremely harsh to people when it comes to health, as it was proven during the so-called pandemic. So, why they aren't being as harsh to diabetics too? After all, the average mortality age of diabetics is from 35 to 64 years, which is way younger than those from cold viruses, which is around 82. Why isn't government protecting the NHS by forcing these people into certain lifestyle? After all, we all pay to sustain most of diabetics directly and indirectly in their conditions, which can be altered and avoided. Do they even know how many people annually die from diabetics compared to cold viruses? If they do know that and do nothing to save them and protect the NHS, then it appears to me like a huge hypocrisy...

One thing should be clear to anyone – the existing order of how the society is being run cannot go on forever without consequences. The society has to change, and changes must be drastic. Unfortunately, no political party as of today offers anything resembling a true solution. Politicians are just so happy to satisfy any demands of the so-called activists, just to get elected. If they don't, the media will be after them as for the media to pretend to be the gate keepers is the easy part. They don't care and don't understand what burden their virtue signalling creates for society.

I recently listened to a discussion on Radio BBC. And there were politicians and presenters discussing how there is a need for help with mental illness on all levels to tens of thousands (if not hundreds) of people. In their mind – government just has to provide them all with decent help... Guess what, the country has only as many people as it has, and most of them have been busy satisfying their previous whims... The levels of demands in Europe are unsustainable. No wonder there are no workers for actual jobs as everybody is helping each other out with things they gave them in the first place with other silly policies...

The overpopulation of the world

Anyway! Let us look at the other numbers, especially at the numbers of populations...

So, we already learned that the whole world has **105 million square kilometres** of habitable land. And the world also has **8 billion people** living on it. That makes the average density in the world around **76 people per square kilometre ON THIS WHOLE HABITABLE LAND**. If we know that **37% of this habitable land** are forests, and they, ideally, should never be touched, then we are left with **66 million square kilometres** of land we are living ON. And in this case, it would leave around **121 people** per square kilometre on this land. If we returned to forests those **20 million square kilometres**, then we would be left with **46 million sq. km** of habitable land for us to live on and which we could use to provide ourselves with food. In this case we would be left with around **174 people** per sq. km.

> *Summary! – The world has **105 million sq. km** of habitable land and with **8 billion people** living on it! That makes density of **76 people living on each sq.km** of this land. Since woodlands have **37%** of all habitable land, then the density of remaining territory is **121 ppl per sq. km**. And if we returned to forests those **20 million sq. km**, then the density on the remaining territory, if the world had **8 billion people** living on it, would be **174 ppl per sq. km**. The number that I am going to use the most in comparisons with densities of individual countries is those **76 people per sq. km.** on all habitable land.*

In all considerations we still have to keep in mind that there are vast areas of the so-called habitable land in places like Siberia, which are only habitable on the paper, as the average weather there is too harsh for most people to live there permanently. And that would bring the total average density per actually habitable land higher. How much exactly? I have no idea! Possibly, some **220 ppl per sq. km**. Who knows! Still, now we have already some numbers to compare the specific density in some countries to the total density on habitable land. And we also know that the world is currently already overpopulated with the existing density... **10 times too many**, in fact.

Now, since the first country that usually comes to our minds (when we are talking about the overpopulation) is China, then let us explore its density also first...

<u>Wikipedia on China:</u>

Area: **9.6 million** sq. km

Population: **1.41 billion**

Average density: **145**

You would be surprised how small this number actually is compared to quite a few other countries. Of course, China has a little secret when it comes to its density.

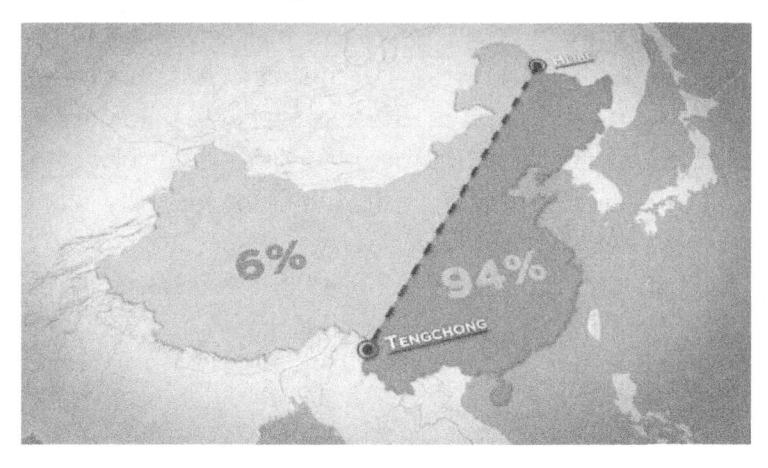

Source: **ReaLifeLore/YouTube**

Yes, **94% if China's population** is living on **43% of its land**. And that raises its actual density in this area to **321** (instead of **145) people**

per sq. km. The thing is – the Western part of China is made out of the highest mountain ranges in the world and of deserts with extremely low precipitation and terrible temperatures in winters and summers. In essence, these areas are very hostile to anything alive.

So, Chinas current density of **321 ppl per sq. km** is around **4.2 times higher** than the existing average number (76 people per sq. km) on all habitable land. However, since the actual number of people that this planet can support without leaving a serious damage to ecosystems most likely is around **10 times smaller** still than those **76** people, then we can conclude that <u>China is at least some **45 times over the limit**</u>.

> **Note!** - *If we returned all territories to forests and were living on **46 million sq.km** of land, and we had these **750 million people** living on it, then it would lead to **16 ppl per sq.km** specifically on those **46 million sq. km**. This number would be around **7 people per sq. km**, if we **had 750 million** people against **105 million sq. km** or all habitable land.*

Either way, China's number is around **45 times too high** when compared to this ideal. If the rest of the world had the same density as China currently has on all of its habitable lands, then right now we would have around **34 billion** people living on our planet. Clearly, that is not sustainable density at all. And China's density is **only 83rd in the world**... Of course, China would have a different place on this list if the habitable land only was used in these calculations... Still, obviously, there are way too many people here.

One of the most densely populated countries today is India.

Wikipedia on India:

Area: **3.3 million** sq. km

Population: **1.43 billion**

Average density: **420**

As you can see, India's territory is around **3 times smaller** than China's, but its population is slightly larger. That leads to nearly **3 times larger** density too, if we use the total density of China. This density of India, however, is only the **30th in the world**... We have to admit though that most of the other countries with extremely high density are rather small, if not tiny. Only some of them are significant, like **Bangladesh**, for instance. There are **170 million** people living in Bangladesh presently, and its density is a staggering **1.3 thousand people per sq. km**... Remember the ideal density of **7 ppl per sq. km**? It makes Bangladesh's density around **182 times too many people** per each sq. km. With this density the world would currently have around **136.5 billion people**... But there are also such countries as **South Korea** (**507** ppl per sq. km), **Netherlands** (**520**), **England** (**434**)..., which all have very high densities too.

Still, the density of India might be the most important one because its total population is so large. But, as I said it previously, the actual density of China is rather **321 people per sq. km**. So, nothing special about India's **420**, right? Well, India also has lands that are not habitable. After all, it has high mountain ranges and valleys with very steep sides, where one can only grow woodlands or feed their cattle. There are also some fairly dry regions and even deserts. With all that in mind, their true density (on the land that is truly habitable) might be somewhere in the region of **600+ per sq. km**. I always wonder - how do they feed themselves, right?

Turns out, India has the largest arable land of all the other countries in the world. Even more than the USA itself, which is a close follower to India. And large masses of India's population are starving or living on a very simple, poor diet. This is how they survive – by keeping huge masses of people in poverty.

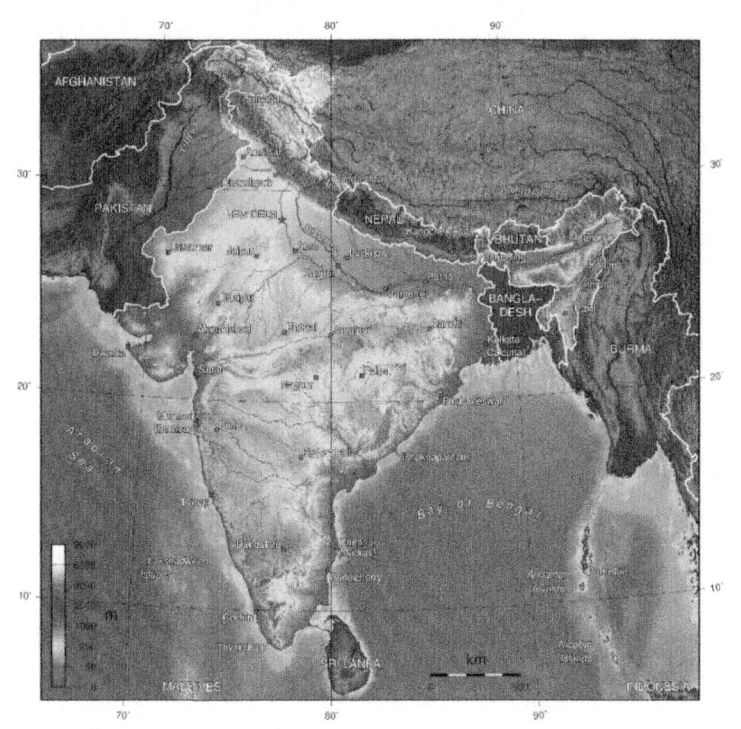

Note! - As you can see in this image, Bangladesh is on the right side, right next to India. It is a very small piece of land (painted dark green in this image) for such a huge population.

Anyway! If the whole world had the density of India, those **420 to 600 ppl per sq. km.**, then we would have **44 to 63 billion people** living on Earth. It is still not bad compared to Bangladesh's **136 billion people.** Remember - the Earth can only comfortably afford under **1 billion** of us tops. So, if I am right about that, and the density of humans on Earth can only be **16 people per sq. km**, then Bangladesh has exceeded it by AT LEAST **182 times** already now...

If the starvation starts, and it definitely will with the current trend of events, then all societies will very quickly turn against each other. In fact, it will lead to unheard violence among communities and countries. Tolerance to anything will fly out of the window. Dark times are upon us! You can mark my words! We have few years tops till it kicks in.

Now, let's take a look at the **United Kingdom**, where some very "decent and caring" politicians keep all doors open for immigration.

Wikipedia on United Kingdom:

Area: **242 thousand** sq. km

Population: **68 million**

Average density: **270**

It seems fairly reasonable, right? After all, **Germany** has **232 people per sq. km.**, and **France** has only **105 (or 121)**. However, when we look specifically at England, the picture is quite different.

Wikipedia on England:

Area: **130 thousand** sq. km

Population: **57 million**

Average density: **434**

Interesting! - If we applied England's density to the whole world, the world would have right now **45 billion people**. That means, England is already around **60 times** over the levels of healthy average population numbers in the world. And this density is way higher than

China has... Remember? – China's density would lead to **34 billion** people and **45 times too high** density...

As we already learned, the UK provides only **60%** of all the food it consumes, and the number of population keeps growing... Yes, from the facts expressed in this book we can conclude that England's ideal population number is closer to **750 thousand**. This number would represent that ideal density in the world with **750 million** people on it!

Now, let us compare England with the most populated country in Europe, the Netherlands...

Wikipedia on the Netherlands:

Area: **41 thousand** sq. km

Population: **17.8 million**

Average density: **520**

I already said that the Netherlands are the second largest food producer in the world. But right now its farmers are fighting hard to keep this production going. There are forces in this world that want to reduce the amount of the food available to people at all costs. What is their goal? Global starvation? I have no idea! One thing is clear – we should be preserving absolutely all food we produce and leave nothing wasted. The food might be very scarce very soon. Any reserves will be welcome.

One thing is clear - this level of population density is way above what should be considered dangerous and unsustainable in a long run. This density of the Netherlands is **6.8 times larger** than the total average current density on our planet. And this density is around **74 times larger** than that healthy world's density of 750 million. With the current density of the Netherlands, the world would have around this density there would be **54.6 billion** people living on this planet. Clearly, absolutely insane, and unsustainable numbers.

Now, Wikipedia on Latvia:

>Area: **64 thousand** sq. km
>
>Population: **1.84 million**
>
>Average density: **29.6**

As you can see, the density of population in Latvia is much lower than in most countries, but still too high. Actually, it is more than 2 times lower than the existing global density (76) on the whole habitable land. However, it is still around **4 times larger** than the possible ideal. If the whole world had the density of population of Latvia, then right now would have around **3 billion** people living on it. So, it isn't that low at all.

When I already finished this book, and even published it, I came across a very telling discussion on Latvia's news website. I realised that the topic of this discussion had to be included here. The title of the show is called "**Spried ar Delfi**" ("Make Decisions with Delfi"**)**, which appeared on **www.delfi.lv.** They were interviewing two officials from different agricultural organizations. The topic of the episode was – **Latvia has been hit by unheard draught, what do we do!**

In essence, they said that due to only 40% of precipitation in April, and only 20% of average anticipated precipitation in May, the crop yield has been severely damaged. Also, they said that far too many fields have failed to produce enough grass for the hay. On some occasions. According to them, there was so little of it that it was no use even to start to cut it. They also said that nobody has seen such a dry spring in Latvia ever, and some farmers in Europe (in this case Germany was mentioned) have been reporting the same problems.

As one of the solutions suggested by them was to start to invest in irrigation systems, as the severity of draughts seem to be growing and are to be expected to be a regular visitor in future. But using groundwaters will only solve one problem in short term and create another one in the long run. As I already mentioned it previously, when we start to pump the ground waters for watering crops, they start to diminish too and rather rapidly. Remember that documentary – **Pumped Dry**? Yes, definitely find it and watch!

On top of that, the role of underground rivers and streams in our ecosystems is very much underexplored, as are the sources of their water. In my view, these underwater rivers are like veins through which the **BLOOD OF EARTH** is flawing. If we drain them, then we could have killed the last bastion of Nature. And them, very likely, even the remaining trees themselves will start to die from draught.

First we have slaughtered around **20 million sq. km**. of Virgin Forests, which led to shortages of precipitation in some places, and changed patterns of precipitation in others. Trees are still surviving from groundwater, but their small number is unable to provide the needed volumes of precipitation. And because of that we don't have enough rain for our crops (and that is A HUGE AND GROWING PROBLEM RIGHT NOW IN THE WHOLE WORLD), which is why we started to use groundwaters to water our crops. But that water down there is disappearing too… Since the draughts keep increasing, and since the crop yields that depend on it will also decrease, we will be forced to use more and more water from underground and overground rivers. But that water isn't returning at the usual volumes as there isn't enough forests. At the same time, the numbers of humans and their prosperity in the world grows. That means, human demand for food and goods grow… But if the existing fields no longer can provide that, it can lead to us being forced to create new ones, right? But where?

The only option is – more Deforestation... **REALLY**???!!! Well, there is absolutely no other choice. But that is suicidal!

If this doesn't sound terrifying to you right now, than you will only change your views when all of this will come true. But that might happen any year from now, including the year when this book is being written – right now is **June of 2023**... Yes, there is a good chance that already in this year we will see the turning point and we will face the terrible consequences of our scientists and politicians having failed us big time. We already know how they failed us miserably with the latest virus of cold, don't we?

Interestingly, this year Latvia experienced some of the coldest frosts in May in recorded history too. One might wonder how can that be, if there is this looming Global Warming, right??? Turns out, Climate Change comes with many different and unexpected changes. Days become hotter; nights become colder. This is similar to the average precipitation, which seemingly has remained the same at least in some places and if we look at the yearly volumes... In reality though there are periods of killer draughts followed by periods of killer rains. And the same is true with temperatures. The average temperature has risen only by **1.2 degrees** Celsius, but the average day temperatures in summer might have risen by some **5 degrees**, while the night temperatures have dropped by some **4**. Do you remember that quote with the temperature fluctuations in deserts? Yes, the colder nights are caused by hotter days and drier air in general.

I have to admit that I don't know exact changes of these temperature swings between days and nights, and these that I just gave you are a pure speculation. But one thing is clear – these changes are happening. And science is silent about them...

Mpemba Effect and climate change...

Do you want to know why temperatures at night are currently lower than they used to be? This might be affected by at least two factors. One of them is lower Relative Humidity..., as higher moisture in air reduces temperatures (keeps the air cooler) during the day and keeps them higher (warmer) at night. And this claim has been confirmed by science...

The other factor that might be affecting these temperature swings between days and nights is known as the Mpemba Effect. Namely, some experiments surprised scientists because it turned out that if you put in a fridge two containers with water, where one of them is slightly warmer then the other, then the warmer one will turn into ice sooner... Namely, it seems that temperature collapse from warmer to colder happens faster and reaches lower temperatures. And the same might be true with air too, possibly because there is water in it too. But that is especially dangerous for countries that are at the same latitudes as Latvia is. Namely (due to this Mpemba Effect), in springs, when orchards and many early plants are in blossoms, the temperatures at night can collapse beyond freezing. It has always been so. Sometimes these spring frosts are not dangerous at all, but sometimes can inflict real harm. Now, however, the temperature falls under freezing levels are more likely, they happen faster, and the frost lasts for longer than it used to be years ago. That leads to collapse of many food sources.

If we add to this problem these extremely dry springs and summers, and too rainy autumns, then it becomes as perfect recipe for a massive crop failure. And even that isn't everything. The disappearing ground waters will come as another blow to our food production lines. We are on a very, very thin ice right now as a humankind, and **it all started with Deforestation.**

If you are in Latvia, politicians will keep saying that the territories of forests have increased significantly in recent decades. Yet, if you are driving along the countryside, you will see so many levelled woodlands that it will give you a feeling of a recent apocalypse. I have heard many people confirming this after they have returned from having visited the places of their origins. Yet, on the paper, Latvia has so much forests as never before. I wonder what we will find in Russia's forests... After all, the disappearance of those forests is doomed to have the effect on whole Europe and Asia...

Now, let's make it more interesting and compare Latvia with another country. For this I chose England. I just found it interesting.

England's territory is nearly perfectly two times larger than Latvia's is, and that makes the comparison easier. So, <u>England</u> has a population of **57 million**, while Latvia has **1.84 million**. If we cut England in two equal parts, then they each would have the same area as Latvia has. And then on each of these parts there would be **28.5 million** people living. <u>The difference between England's 28.5 and Latvia's 1.84 is **15.5 times**</u>... Namely, Latvia has **15.5 times less** people per the same area than England has. And I already told you that Latvia itself is also overpopulated. Of course, those are average numbers, as there are regions with much higher and much lover densities. Either way, with Latvia's density England would have **3.68 million** people living in it.

To understand the density difference better, think of an average 3-bedroom house in which 1 person lives. That would represent Latvia. And right next to it there would be identical house with 15 people and a baby living in it. They would be able to manage it..., but the difference of density between these two houses would be huge and very obvious to anyone who would have been in both of them. And this is what I can feel on a daily basis while living in England and having come from Latvia. This over-crowdedness is slightly terrifying. I see it everywhere. It scares me, especially when I think about this overpopulated world and how it led to the Climate Change, how the food production becomes more and more challenging.

The world keeps getting increasingly overcrowded, our prosperity grows, and with it grows our demand for goods. Clearly, the world is on the course of collapse already, mainly because of the levels of Deforestation, but politicians (and, sadly, scientists too) fail to see the problem. As I said, to provide with the full scale of goods all people on this planet we would need <u>around **320 million sq. km** of habitable land</u>. But the world only has **105 in total**... We are in a very grim place right now, and that is mainly because of overpopulation, which is at least 10 times too high already. With the existing numbers we simply use way more water than the nature is able replace, even if all the forests were restored.

I have said this and will keep saying – go and ask any UK's politician this one question – ***How much, in their view, would be too many people living in Britain?*** After all, there should be a clear number after which it becomes dangerously overcrowded. And they all will fail to answer this question, as that would reduce their chances of being elected. So, this is where we are. We have politicians who are so desperate to get elected that they don't care about how their actions might lead to a huge disaster in future, as long as they get into power today. THIS ISN'T WHAT DEMOCRACY IS ABOUT, THIS ISN' T WHAT DEMOCRACY WAS MEANT TO BE ABOUT. And most definitely, this isn't a good and sane leadership. Having said that, I believe that the main blame in this insanity is on shoulders of mass media, on journalists, who so desperately wanted to be better than the pope in the Catholic Church is, that they started to blame and shame anyone who even indicates, that there might be something wrong with the growing numbers of British population. Those who remained sane, like **Nigel Farage**, have been vilified by the self-appointed as "the only correct and good media", like all at **BBC** and the likes.

Because of English language, open door policies, and fairly high tolerance levels all around in Britain, the UK has become a magnet to many poorer societies from all over the world. And that is especially true with countries which used to be British colonies, and where large number of people already speak English. Those are countries like **India, Pakistan, Nigeria, etc**... The total number of population in these **3 countries** alone is around **1.9 billion**... If only **1%** of them moved to Britain, it would increase British population by **19 million**. Everyone knows that there are much <u>more than 1% of people in these countries that desperately wish to come over</u>. But with the increase by this 1%, the total number of people in Britain would reach **87 million**. Ask those politicians (and media), especially those who keep promoting this "all doors open" policies, and also ask those environmentalists who hate CO2 but have nothing against the overpopulation this question – can the UK sustain such a large number of people (87 million) without serious damage to environment along with serious danger of being unable to feed them at some point when there will be food crises in the world? If they say yes, ask them how exactly they see this and aren't they worried about looming food shortages all over the globe. If they say no, then as them how they see it being stopped.

In real life, when these questions are presented to them, they all will turn away from you and start shaming you by calling you a racist or something. Answering a sane and legitimate question isn't on their agenda. It is easier to hate CO2 alone and pretend that reducing it will solve any of our problems... But it won't!

Conclusion!

At this point it should be clear to any reader that we are very close to reaching irreparable damage to our planet. Actually, I think that we might be past it, but the consequences of that are still on the way as they come with a certain dely. The fact that disaster hasn't hit us yet doesn't prove its not coming. With the tipping point it is as it is with **avalanches** - the problems (the mass of snow in case of avalanches) keeps growing, and we can observe them doing that. But for a long period nothing happens. And then, at one moment, the tipping weight of the burden is reached, and a huge mass of snow comes crashing down in one devastating movement. The same might be true when the global ecological disaster will hit our planet. And nobody seems to be too bothered. Everybody is focusing on the CO2 emissions, and only partly addressing Deforestation.

When it comes to overpopulation, a vast majority of politicians and scientists even declare, that we actually need much more people on this planet... Clearly, sanity has abandoned these shores. Madmen are leading us right towards the abyss and they are encouraging us to speed up towards it... So, what do we do? Is there anything we actually can do to turn the tides? I am not sure about that. It could be that "**this avalanche**" will inevitably come and hit us. And through this the Nature will balance everything out by itself. We have been slaughtering the Nature for so long without any response from it. Now it's HER TIME to deliver the blow back to us... And it will. All we can do now is fasten your seatbelts and wait for the moment of impact. After all, stupidity is worse than a crime, as criminal at least understand that he is doing something wrong. That means, they can stop. Stupid people, however, lead into disaster by singing songs and organizing feasts to celebrate their achievements in this, and laughing at those who warn them of imminent danger.

There is thing I probably didn't explain fully about those **8 million people** that this planet would be able to sustain even if we restored **20 million sq. km of forests**. I said that all of these people should be fully vegans. And the numbers show that it could work, right? In reality, that's not so simple. The thing is – such population would be using every single inch of the available arable land for food, and they all would just get by in terms of food supplies. If the world experienced one bad year in terms of crop yield, they all would suffer. On top of that, they still would be using quite a lot of water and wood. If you remember, the statistics say that the whole humankind currently uses **10 billion tons** of water every day. And from all those lost forests we only would get back around **137 million tons** per day. That's **73 times** the difference. What that means? It means that the water consumption by such huge population numbers is way bigger than the Nature can restore. Of course, we could reduce our consumption, and the rest will be returned by forests. Still, that won't be enough in a long run! We simply cannot live on the border of impossible. We need some space for manoeuvres in case something goes wrong. And we need much more than 10 % of safety cushion. Also, it is highly unlikely that the whole world will be happy to become vegans.

As you can see, in order to sustain 8 billion people we should be perfect with our food growth and consumption, and also perfect with water and wood consumption. Clearly, anyone who lives on a border of the possible, sooner or later will fail with something. And that means, the world might breath easily only if we reduced those numbers of ours really significantly. As I said, my estimate is **750 million** tops.

∗∗∗

Now a few words to those people who still believe in the **God Creator** of **Abrahamic Religions**. Famously, God so much loved the world/humans, that He gave his only begotten son to be sacrificed for our sins… To me this all sounds like a pure and clear lie which only the blind are unable to recognize. After all, it should be abundantly clear that our planet is on its way to die. And that is 100% because of human activities and our sheer numbers. This will lead to global starvation and enormous suffering very soon. So, my question to all people who believe in this "caring God" is this – Tell me, why this God failed to explain these things to us, and why is He silent now, if He cares so much about us? Either this God doesn't exist, or He is illiterate and has no clue about anything of this, or He has abandoned humans altogether and long time ago. So, maybe it is time we abandon Him too…

Humans shouldn't interfere in climate change apart from restoring it to the original state

Note! - This is a very important chapter of this book, as here you will learn about why we shouldn't take words of scientists, environmentalists and different PhD holders for granted, when it comes to saving our planet, and finding the right culprits of problems and also solutions.

Ever since humans realised that our activities are damaging to the climate, we have started to look for ways to fix it. Unfortunately, our understanding of how to fix it is highly delusional. Some of us have even realised this in other fields and coined a saying – **we cannot fix a problem by doing the same things that led us into it in the first place**. Yet, this is exactly what humans are doing with respect to climate change when attempting to fix it.

Yes, we are trying to fix climate problems with further interference in the climate. And no, we have no intention of fixing the problems with afforestation and depopulation. **We are going to fight not the causes, but the consequences of climate change**. It doesn't help anything. For instance, humans are talking about **CO2 capture**, **cloud seeding**, and other methods that are meant to help address climate change.

In this chapter, I will explain why all these approaches will have catastrophic consequences. Before we examine them, I would like you to learn about a few attempts by humans to solve certain problems by interfering with natural processes, which had severe consequence.

For the sake of this book, I would like to discuss two very well-known cases that are recognised worldwide. The first is about wolves in Yellowstone Park, and the second is about sparrows in China.

The miracle that saved Yellowstone Park:

the reintroduction of wolves

Famously, **Yellowstone National Park** in the **USA** is the very first such protected area in known human history. Who knows, perhaps without this pioneering action, no other nation would have realised the importance of the natural beauty and uniqueness of certain areas, which would have vanished from the face of the Earth forever if not protected. Unfortunately, many countries in the world today are so overpopulated that they cannot even afford 'the luxury of national parks".

Yellowstone National Park was established in 1872. By the beginning of the 20th century, the wolf population in the area had already been wiped out. European settlers were exterminating bison and wolf populations at an alarming rate, often just for sport. Wolves already had a bad reputation in the minds of humans, which made them a target and 'fair game.' In Yellowstone, they were killed to protect farm animals. No one was bothered about wiping them out completely.

More than 120 years after the creation of Yellowstone Park, it was decided to reintroduce wolves to it. As usual, there was an outcry against this idea, including from many environmentalists, who claimed it would disrupt the delicate balance of the ecosystem. This is how we learned that, despite these individuals often calling themselves scientists and holding PhDs, they are frequently delusional about the consequences of such actions. The same applies when these environmentalists discuss the benefits of afforestation.

Amazingly, they will glue themselves to tarmac to protest against oil consumption, yet they will reject even the suggestion of discussing the role of forests and the need for global afforestation to restore the planet to its original state. Yes, they are delusional, blind, and deaf, and so we cannot allow them to lead the fight against climate change.

Wolves have been a natural part of America's fauna and flora for an indefinite period. Nowadays, even environmentalists have realised that wolves serve not only as the 'hygienists of the woods', removing weak and sick animals, but also maintain a great balance between different species. To the surprise of even the biggest supporters of their return, wolves also restored balance to plant life and helped protect the geography of the area. Nobody expected that.

So, what happened after the wolves were reintroduced to Yellowstone National Park?

Wolves were reintroduced to the park in the 1990s. Within two decades, the changes they caused to the park were mind-blowing — in a positive way.

Without wolves, the deer population had exploded in the park. They were grazing on everything in their path, and had no natural enemies, apart from some hyenas, which weren't too dangerous to the deer anyway.

So, the first thing that happened was the reduction of the deer population. The deer stopped visiting areas of the park where they were most unprotected from wolves. In these places, a very unique plant life returned and began to flourish. Next, quite a few trees returned, which further helped the return of many bird species.

Next, wolves purged coyotes from the area, which allowed the return of small animals, like different types of mice, rabbits, and even beavers. Beavers began to build dams, which created a habitat for even more species. Everything seemed to have gained a second breath. Everything started to flourish.

The most interesting part of the changes was the stabilization of soil around riverbanks. It happened because trees started to grow there. That, too, was a change that nobody expected. Erosion of the riverbanks stopped, and a new stability and prosperity began for many species. Everything in that area sprung back to incredible life, all because of the return of wolves, who have always been a part of the landscape.

This story is just one of many famous examples in human history that prove human intervention leads to the degradation of all forms of life on Earth. We must stop that intervention and start realising that without healthy natural cycles, there can be no life on Earth at all. We all know, and this has been officially declared by scientists, that around 60% of all species on Earth are currently in danger if everything continues as it is. Yet, nothing changes. We keep increasing the human population and continue to encourage the production of more and more children... The entire scientific community is like the main crowd from the movie "**Don't Look Up!**" People just keep shouting – **Don't Tell Us About That!... We Don't Want To Know!... Let's Party Instead!...**

Before we move on to the main topic – the fact that human intervention in the climate, with ideas like **CO2 capturing**, **cloud seeding**, and **others**, is only making things worse – I would like to look at another famous story of human intervention in nature that turned sour. That is the story of how China sought to increase their crop yield by getting rid of sparrows.

JURIS BOGDANOVS

China's attempt to increase crop yields by killing off sparrows turned sour

In 1957, China started a campaign to eradicate mosquitoes, flies, rats, and, above all, sparrows. Sparrows seemed to be the easiest targets of all. They were blamed for robbing people of the fruits of their labour, i.e., the crop yield. A massive campaign was organised to disturb, purge, and kill off as many sparrows as possible. And all of this was driven by good intentions, to ensure that people received all the grain from their labour.

People kept making noises with drums and other sound-producing equipment to keep the birds in the air, until they were so exhausted that they fell to the ground. The Chinese were taking them away in small lorries, as the number of killed sparrows was mind-blowing..

It was a time when humans still believed they were the rulers of the world, and that nature had to bend to any of their whims. Keep in mind that the story of Yellowstone was, in effect, of the same nature...

Initially, after nearly all the sparrows were exterminated, there was great joy all around. And at least in the first year, it seemed to have helped with crop yield. Unfortunately, when the sparrows were wiped out, all kinds of pests began to thrive. Their population, much like the deer population in Yellowstone, exploded.

One of the worst insect population explosions was with locusts. There were so many of them that they annihilated everything in their path. The damage they caused to the crop yield was far greater than that caused by the sparrows. It was an ecological disaster that led to a terrible famine. It is said that up to 50 million people died from starvation as a result of the locust disaster.

Having realized their mistake, the Chinese government asked Russia (then the Soviet Union) to help with the reintroduction of sparrows.

They brought around 250,000 sparrows from Russia, stabilizing the situation.

One might assume that these two stories—and they are far from the only ones demonstrating human folly—would make people think twice about the consequences of their actions when attempting to control nature. You would be surprised to learn that this isn't the case; with current global actions aimed at limiting climate change, we are repeating the same, if not even greater, mistakes.

Let's examine them.

The dangers of Geoengineering or Climate Engineering

First of all, I am sure you will be surprised to learn how many methods are being used to interfere with or mitigate the effects of climate change. You will also be surprised to learn how often and in how many countries these methods are already being practiced, simply because they can...

It is terrifying how few scientists are warning about these dangers and how regularly the voices of those who do are ignored. I've already mentioned this, but we literally live in a world that 'doesn't want to look up'!

Cloud seeding

> **Wikipedia** <u>on 'cloud seeding'</u>: *Cloud seeding is a type of weather modification that aims to change the amount or type of precipitation, mitigate hail or disperse fog. The usual objective is to increase rain or snow, either for its own sake or to prevent precipitation from occurring in days afterward.*

*Cloud seeding is undertaken **by dispersing substances into the air** that serve as **cloud condensation** or **ice nuclei**. Common agents include **silver iodide, potassium iodide**, and **dry ice**, with hygroscopic materials like **table salt** gaining popularity due to their ability to attract moisture. Techniques vary from static seeding, which encourages **ice particle formation in supercooled clouds** to increase precipitation, to **dynamic seeding**, designed to enhance convective cloud development through the release of latent heat.*

If you just look at this description, it seems fairly innocent, meant only to benefit certain societies at certain times. No harm done, right?! You must have spotted that there are several methods for causing rain in situations where there would be no rain naturally.

For the sake of this book, these methods aren't even important. What is important, however, is the fact that these practices lead to rain in conditions where the relative humidity is already too low for rain to occur naturally. But that means the already drier air is made even drier by this cloud seeding... And that means the chances of naturally occurring rain are reduced even more in the near future.

The worst thing about this method is that those ill effects, most likely, will affect other nearby countries, not the one using them. Namely, if somebody is actively doing cloud seeding, say, in Saudi Arabia, then it might cause severe periods of drought in Yemen, Iran, Iraq, Oman, etc. And the likelihood is that those side effects will play out to the east of the country doing the cloud seeding, as the atmosphere generally moves eastward around the world.

Also, and the most diligent readers might have already realized this, cloud seeding will inevitably lead to higher temperatures and even heatwaves, simply because it further decreases relative humidity.

Interestingly, with all the money Saudi Arabia has, they aren't investing in afforestation of the region, which would help solve many problems with droughts in the long run, but instead, they are making things worse by applying cloud seeding.

"I wish Saudi Arabia were the only country using this method. It is no secret that to a very great extent and for quite some time, the same practice has been employed by the USA, India, China, and many other countries. The most tragic consequences would occur if India were using it, as that would affect China's weather. If Pakistan were using it, it would affect India, causing droughts there. And so on... This is how Weather Engineering becomes a Weather Weapon, because you can inflict real damage to their crop yield with it..."

Let's look at some news stories involving cloud seeding.

China, China, China... Turns out China even has a Weather Modification Office.

Wikipedia:

> *The Beijing Weather Modification Office is a unit of the Beijing Meteorological Bureau tasked with* **weather control** *in* **Beijing**, *and* **its surrounding areas**, *including* **parts of Hebei** *and* **Inner Mongolia**.
>
> *The Beijing Weather Modification* **Office form a part of China's nationwide weather control effort**, *believed to be* **the world's largest**; *it* **employs 37,000** *people nationwide, who seed clouds by* <u>firing rockets</u> *and* <u>shells loaded with silver iodide</u> *into them. According to Zhang Qiang, head of the Office, cloud seeding increased precipitation in Beijing by about one-eighth in 2004.*

From CNN World:

China is seeding clouds to replenish its shrinking Yangtze River

Hong Kong/CNN

By Shawn Deng, Wayne Chang, Simone McCarthy and Reuters, CNN/ Thu August 18, 2022

Chinese planes are firing rods into the sky to bring more rainfall to its crucial Yangtze River, which has dried up in parts, as swaths of the nation fall into drought and grapple with the worst heat wave on record.

Several regions on the Yangtze have launched weather modification programs, but with cloud cover too thin, operations in some drought-ravaged parts of the river's basin have remained on standby.

The Ministry of Water Resources said in a notice on Wednesday that drought throughout the Yangtze river basin was "adversely affecting drinking water security of rural people and livestock, and the growth of crops."

As you can see, severe droughts are affecting everyone everywhere. Who knows, maybe these droughts are caused by earlier cloud seeding in the western parts of China... And India's cloud seeding projects only added fuel to the fire. Yet, nobody acknowledges the possibility of a correlation here...

Let's go to the next article.

India.

From **www.routers.com**

Indian scientists hope cloud seeding can clean Delhi's toxic air

By Shivam Patel/November 9, 2023

Indian scientists plan to seed clouds for the first time to trigger heavy rain in some areas of New Delhi, hoping this will be enough to tackle the smog gripping the world's most polluted capital for a week, the project's head said on Thursday.

Scientists expect some cloud cover over the city around Nov. 20 and are hoping this will be large enough - and with high enough moisture content - to trigger heavy rain via seeding with salts, said Manindra Agrawal, a scientist at the Indian Institute of Technology at Kanpur, who is leading the trial.

The project, estimated to cost 10 million rupees ($120,000) for 100 square kilometres (38.6 square miles), would involve spraying into clouds a mix of salts that include silver iodine, Agrawal said.

The strange thing is, nobody in India is talking about the terrible situation with overpopulation and deforestation... Yet...

Let's move on to other counties.

Indonesia.

From **www.nst,com**

> ***Indonesia prepares cloud seeding strategy to fight forest fires***
>
> *By Bernama - March 3, 2024*
>
> *Indonesia's Ministry of Environment and Forestry, together with key stakeholders, is gearing up to implement a cloud seeding strategy to fight forest and land fires that will start this month.*
>
> *Forest and Land Fire Control director Thomas Nifinluri emphasised the importance of this approach following the recent fire incidents after the monsoon season, particularly in Riau Province.*
>
> *He stated, "This year, our focus is to update the cloud seeding plan with the meteorological agency, BMKG, and ensure readiness in seed material, aircraft, and weather analysis," as quoted by local news outlet, Media Indonesia.*

As you can see, they are preparing for a very serious cloud seeding operations. The sad truth is, the more cloud seeding is being applied around the globe, the drier is the air and the larger chance of wildfires, that will be completely uncontrollable.

Indonesia, the Philippines, and other countries are surrounded by oceans and seas. I don't believe they have experienced such large and regular wildfires as there are now. The same applies to countries like Russia. In all these countries, forests are being annihilated at a great speed. Even in Australia, this is true. And yet, not a single person is asking to restore forests there. The country is drying out because woodlands have been nearly annihilated.

https://vstats.medium.com/

Update: Animal agriculture drives 79% of deforestation in Australia.

Rearing livestock for food and fibre is responsible for more than three-quarters of forest clearing across the country.

CAUSES OF DEFORESTATION
BY ACTIVITY IN AUSTRALIA (2016-2020)

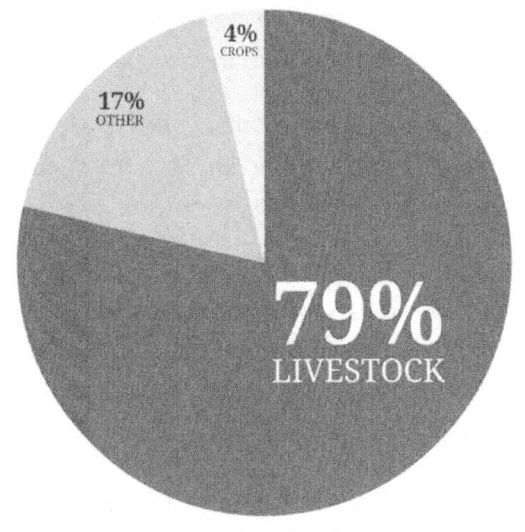

- 4% CROPS
- 17% OTHER
- 79% LIVESTOCK

Data: Australian Government Department of Industry, Science, Energy and Resources, *National Inventory Report Volume 2* (2022), 296-97.

MADE BY VSTATS. FOR MORE INFORMATION: VSTATS.SUBSTACK.COM

Have you ever seen how much woodland has been removed from the Australian landscape over several centuries? It's terrifying. No wonder they are experiencing all those increasing periods of droughts and wildfires. They've even decided to reduce the damage of wildfires by... removing all trees and bushes within certain distances from homes to protect them in case of fire. Amazing...

Next image shows how large territories of forests have been annihilated.

From: **https://forestsandclimate.org.au/national-overview/**

National Overview

By 2009 – 70% of Australia's remaining forests were degraded from logging

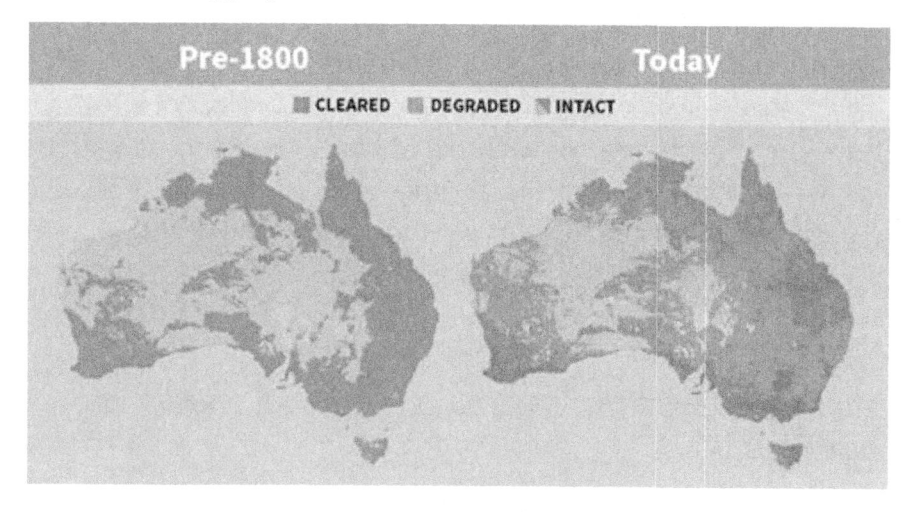

Unsustainable logging and clearing continued up to and beyond the catastrophic 2019-20 fires when 8.19 million hectares of native forest burnt across several states, NSW being worst affected having 5.014 million hectares burnt

You would assume that they learned the lesson... No way! Look how this article ends. They are still thinking about how to stop deforestation, and afforestation isn't even on their lips yet...

Australia must legislate total protection of all that remains of our native forests. With full legislative protection from logging and clearing a national forest restoration programme can commence. Australia must stand firm to demand such protection for native forests, not only on this continent but globally. This affects us all.

Based on the previous picture, in 1800, nearly 50% of Australia was covered by forests. Today, only around 19% remains. These 19% represent approximately 147 million hectares or 1.47 million square kilometres. From this, we can deduce that around 2.4 million square kilometres of forests have been lost since Europeans began settling there. This area is similar to nearly 50% of the entire European Union, which is around 4.2 million square kilometres. Even Alaska is only 1.7 million square kilometres. This represents a massive loss of forests for the entire continent and possibly the whole globe. It definitely affects relative humidity, making the air drier. Additionally, cloud seeding exacerbates the situation, affecting the whole world. It's no wonder wildfires are raging globally nowadays.

From:

https://www.weatherzone.com.au/news/cloud-seeding-in-australia/713971

Cloud seeding in Australia

Ashleigh Lange/27 Jul 2022

Cloud seeding is used in parts of Australia to enhance rain, snowfall and water security.

You simply cannot make this stuff up. We damage our climate by cutting too many forests, which leads to drier air. But drier air leads to higher temperatures and less rain, more frequent and larger and longer wildfires. And to solve the problem caused by drier air, we make it even drier by cloud seeding... We are a suicidal humankind after all. But try to tell anyone that the world is overpopulated and this has led to deforestation of unheard levels and climate change, and everyone will instantly do their best to silence you.

I could go on and on with this, but it should already be abundantly clear that cloud seeding only adds fuel to the fire.

Cloud brightening

The cloud seeding and cloud brightening activities have given rise to conspiracy theories about the **'chemtrails.'** However, the BBC seems very happy and enthusiastic about any human intervention into natural cycles. I recommend one of their articles to you.

From: **https://www.bbc.co.uk/news/articles/c98qp79gj4no**

> ***Conspiracy theories swirl about geo-engineering, but could it help save the planet?***
>
> *21 July 2024/ Simon King/Lead Weather Presenter*
>
> *If we can't control rising global temperatures by drastically cutting carbon emissions, could something called geo-engineering be a way to cool the planet?*
>
> *In what is already a multi-billion-dollar industry, scientists around the world, including in the UK, are researching geo-engineering - ways of manipulating the climate to tackle global warming.*
>
> *Some experts are concerned there are too many risks associated with it, fearing it could mess with global weather patterns or actually warm some regions, not cool them.*
>
> *As the industry grows, so have conspiracy theories. BBC Weather has seen a large increase in social media comments around geo-engineering since January, accusing us of covering up secret projects and wrongly blaming geo-engineering for the cool and wet weather we've recently had.*
>
> *...*

Some geo-engineering ideas include reflecting sunlight back out to space to cool Earth. The most advanced area of geo-engineering is direct air carbon capture with small-scale facilities in operation across Europe, the US and Canada. These currently remove around 10,000 tonnes of carbon dioxide a year, meaning it would need massively scaling up to make any difference to the roughly 35 billion tonnes we emit globally.

"We need to start to think about other things that we can do in order to limit any further warming," says Professor Liz Bentley, chief executive of the Royal Meteorological Society. "That's where geo-engineering starts to become an interesting discussion."

How geo-engineering could cool the atmosphere

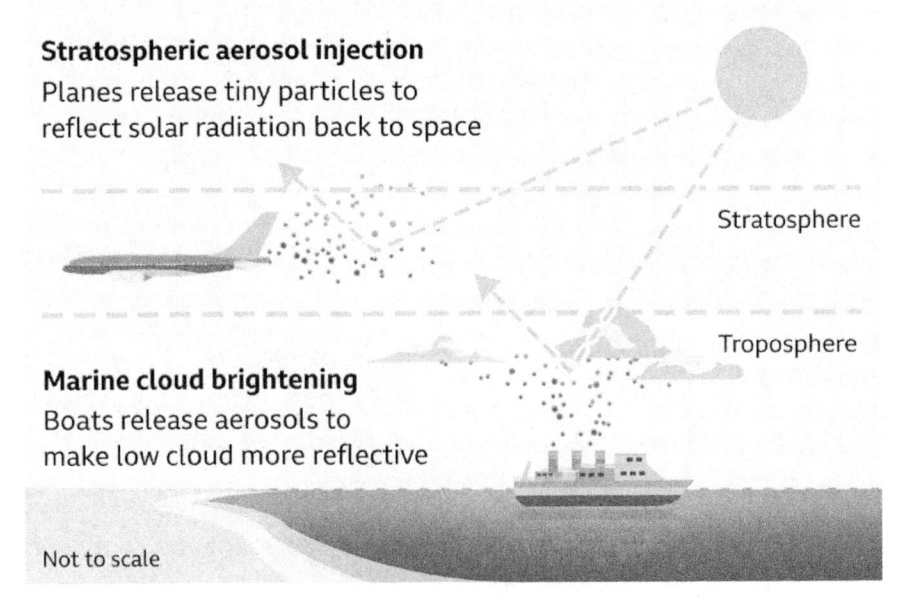

Stratospheric aerosol injection
Planes release tiny particles to reflect solar radiation back to space

Stratosphere

Troposphere

Marine cloud brightening
Boats release aerosols to make low cloud more reflective

Not to scale

Researchers are studying two kinds of solar radiation management: marine cloud brightening and stratospheric aerosol injection.

Marine cloud brightening involves spraying very fine saltwater from a boat towards low-level clouds above the ocean to enhance their brightness and reflectivity.

Modelling has shown that if you were to spray a large area - around 4% of the ocean - near the equator and brighten clouds, the combination of more cloud and consequently a lower sea surface temperature beneath it could have worldwide impacts.

Our atmosphere is complex, has no borders and behaves like a fluid. You may have come across the 'butterfly effect' where if a butterfly were to flutter its wings in Mexico, it can bring rain to the UK. While in reality that is a big leap, it highlights how weather is connected all over the world.

...

Stratospheric tech development

The technology to perform marine cloud brightening on a small scale with fans and sprayers already exists, but the other method of solar radiation management - stratospheric aerosol injection - would need greater advances to have the desired impact.

This method of geo-engineering involves artificially adding aerosols such as sulphate into the stratosphere, which extends from 6-12 miles (10-20km) to 31 miles (50km) above the Earth. These aerosols would reflect some solar radiation, reducing the amount reaching our planet's surface and theoretically cause a global cooling.

As you can see, humans are eager to find a quick fix without changing their bad habits and without knowing what potential side effects this fix will cause in the future. It is similar to trying to fix our addiction to overeating by taking some drugs on top of that so that the food doesn't stick to our belly in the form of fat. We would do anything but the right thing. Unfortunately, the world is at the edge of the cliff right now. There will be no safe place to escape when the whole trouble starts...

CO2 capturing

"I don't know whether you spotted it in the previous quote, but one of the methods currently applied to mitigate the effects of climate change is CO2 capturing. Let us read that quote one more time:

> *The most advanced area of geo-engineering is direct air carbon capture with small-scale facilities in operation across Europe, the US and Canada. These currently remove around 10,000 tonnes of carbon dioxide a year, meaning it would need massively scaling up to make any difference to the roughly 35 billion tonnes we emit globally.*

This method is the closest to those stories of Yellowstone's wolves and China's sparrows. Only, it might be close to impossible to return that captured CO2 back into the air later, when the consequences of this mistake become clear.

CO2 is food for plants and trees. CO2 is even stored in the trunks of trees. If we take CO2 out of the air, then there will be less food for trees when we finally wake up and decide to restore forests. And remember, we have to restore around 20 million sq. km of forests... That will need a lot of CO2...

Now, the most important question - WHAT TO DO to save the world?

First of all, keep in mind that we are already three times too short of habitable land needed to supply the existing 8 billion people with all possible foods. And thanks to human activities that lead to deforestation of our planet, we might be facing a worldwide drought in a few years' time when most crop yields will fail. Not if, but when. The war in Ukraine has only added to food insecurities all around the world. This is not the time for conflicts. **THIS WAR SHOULD BE STOPPED AT ALL COSTS**. WE HAVE AN ENORMOUS PROBLEM IN OUR HANDS TO SOLVE AND IT SHOULD BE DONE RIGHT NOW. WE ALL WILL DIE IF WE DON'T.

Also keep in mind that no one can help us if we aren't willing to do our part, especially now as we are most likely already past the tipping point. Now we can only reduce the severity of this hard landing and hope that we will avoid the death of our planet altogether. And no, it is not up to everyone individually. This approach doesn't work. The measures to save our planet can only work if they are imposed on people. This is because the vast majority of people, if we leave it to individuals, will always declare that it is not their problem, and they will carry on as usual...

As I said, this planet can only safely sustain between 500 million to 1 billion people at any given time. This is because nature needs space to breathe, sustain itself, and keep itself in a healthy balance. It cannot survive if someone is damaging it at a faster rate than it can recover. Whether you like it or not, we will have to learn to live with less—all of us! That time is rapidly approaching. Nobody will escape that. Nobody! So, it's better we push ourselves to this strict discipline earlier, or the natural cycles will push us there in a much harsher way.

One thing that makes this prospect of worldwide starvation even closer is the oppression of farmers all around the world. Not many know this, but farmers in Europe are being forced to stop farming and to use fewer chemicals for their plants. Combined with the mood of war in Europe, this takes the problem at hand to the next level. Not only are we in danger of losing crops to droughts and floods (another side effect of climate change or drying out lands), but we also reduce our own ability to produce food through the illiterate actions of our so-called political leaders. One cannot make this all up. Who needs enemies, right? Sometimes it seems that our civilization is so short-sighted and, frankly, stupid, that it deserves to go through the upcoming suffering and deserves to be annihilated by our own hands.

One thing should be abundantly clear: we need to restore woodlands all around the world and significantly reduce our numbers and greed. Otherwise, our planet will be destroyed. Some extreme consequences are unavoidable already. We will see the changes. What we can do now is this: we can reduce the length and strength of the forthcoming pain by starting to restore the amount and quality of woodlands.

Afforestation is easier and faster to achieve than any of those **insane 'zero CO2 emissions' goals**. Nature will deal with the CO2 by itself if we allow (and help) the woodlands and peatlands to grow back. But we have to start helping nature, and we have to do it RIGHT NOW. We also have to start reducing the number of people in the world along with reducing our consumption. WE HAVE TO ACT NOW AND DO ALL THE THINGS MENTIONED BELOW ALL AT THE SAME TIME!

Before moving to what to do to save the world, let's take a look at what we shouldn't be doing ...

"I already explained that we shouldn't be interfering with the processes of nature. We already have a long list of things we've screwed up in the past while interfering. And right now, our actions are like crazy experiments with our own survival at stake. Yet, we just cannot stop ourselves...

One thing that I didn't mention here is the transition to the so-called renewable energy with all those solar panels and wind generators. They have their own negative impact on nature with little to no benefits. By focusing on these projects, we are losing precious time needed for saving the planet by replanting forests.

The main topic of this part, however, is about the obsession with EVs (electric vehicles). These vehicles not only won't save anything, but they will make humankind extremely immobile and vulnerable in the event of some global problems. Just think about the chance of extreme heat or cold. Those vehicles discharge really fast in those conditions. How would you escape from a state consumed by wildfires in an electric vehicle? Mission impossible!

In one radio LBC discussion, an EV driver called in. He has a business in transporting people. He bought an 8-seater, fully electric vehicle. On a hot day, with 8 passengers and air conditioning on, his car was able to do only 80 km (or miles) from a full charge. This is not sustainable.

Now think about the charging stations for these EVs. These vehicles need longer and more frequent charges. So, to satisfy all demand with the same number of cars as we currently have, every country would need around three times more charging stations than we currently have petrol stations. I don't believe any of that is ever possible.

THINGS WE HAVE TO DO TO TURN THE TIDES OF SELF-ANNIHILATION!

1. Start afforestation and protection of the existing Virgin Forests. Start to develop them back at speeds significantly faster than cutting them down.

2. Drastically reduce the consumption of wood by limiting use of papers, wooden packaging etc.

3. Start reducing numbers of people on this planet by introducing One Child Policy everywhere on the globe till sustainable levels are achieved. Yes, it will lead to older society in general, and the retirement ages will have to be changed significantly too. But the cost of not doing it is much higher and more painful.

4. Stop urbanisation and globalization. These lead to longer supply chains and, for that reason, larger consumption.

5. Start to restore the swamps and peatlands.

6. Drastically reduce consumption of meat production.

7. Start to create conserved food reserves and waste absolutely nothing.

8. Start rationing of food rather earlier than later, as we should do it while there is abundance of it instead of when it is clear that we don't have enough anymore.

9. Consumption philosophy and claims about economical "growth, growth, growth" should be stopped. It leads to absurd decisions. We will have to abandon fake employment created by greed and desire to have increasingly more and all the time new products, as that leads to destruction of our planet.

1. Start afforestation and protection of the existing Virgin Forests. Start to develop them back at speeds significantly faster than cutting them down.

Yes, first of all we have to do everything in our power to plant as many trees as we can, and then make sure more green mass of plants is being grown back than we are consuming in any given year. AND IT SHOULD START NOW! We should never have taken more than the Nature can produce back. Without that we are ruining the natural balance of the Nature and that leads to collapse of the whole system. Virgin Forests should all be preserved and new territories for developing Virgin Forests dedicated and planting started immediately. Absolutely every single person on our planet should become a part of this afforestation. And to achieve that, all methods should be used, including enforcing by the state. We need to change our planet from losing woodlands to growing them back. The most important thing (once again) – the Earth should have more mass of greenery and wood than it is taken from it every year, as the larger territories planted versus territories cut means nothing. Deforestation must be reversed immediately. Forget the CO_2 emissions for the time being. These emissions will be helpful for forests to grow back. Larger CO_2 levels will make it faster. CO_2 is our friend with this.

Another thing we can do is by stopping to move our lawns. The thing is - all plants are contributing to the humidity of the air. Territories around our houses (where we often like to keep that grass extremely low), when taken together, are fairly huge. As a planet we are in place where every little helps. It is better to let your grass grow and do its job than to buy electric car. Electric cars don't help anything. But with grass it will be a real and nearly immediate help. We like our lawns moved very short as it looks great and looked after, right? And then we start to water them... Often, for that we are using groundwater. What a stupid way to ruin natural cycles of water. The grass should only be cut when it becomes overgrown and yellow, which effectively means – it doesn't do any job anymore. The saddest thing with these lawns is that some people remove them completely and replace them with that plastic grass. It looks smooth and looked after and you don't have to do anything to keep it that way, right? At the same time it is a blow to the Nature. This should be stopped.

> **Important reminder!** – Yes, the world is getting hotter, and yes, the CO2 levels are rising. But these things are very good for the growth to all plants. The only thing that slows plants growing in this situation, including crops and forests, is the lack of water. So, naturally, we should ask ourselves – **Where does the water in air come from, right?** Turns out, significant amount of it comes from plants. FROM ALL KINDS OF PLANTS! Plants moisturise the atmosphere, making sure the air has so high humidity that the water can no longer stay there and starts to come down in a form of rain. Also, high humidity stops drying out processes, which are very much the concern right now all over the planet, including drying off glaciers and polar caps.
>
> But these cycles of water have been heavily damaged now by Deforestation. The sad thing is, scientists keep talking about the CO2 levels, and how increase of them will lead to severe consequences in 2100, but the lost forests are only a little concern to them.. Guess what!? If we carry on with Deforestation as we currently do, there might be nothing left on this planet by 2050, let alone 2100. We don't have that time.
>
> It is embarrassing how blind science community is to these facts about the role of trees in humidity levels, water cycles and temperatures on Earth. Yes, they talk about lost biodiversity

*because of lost forests. Yes, they talk about trunks of trees being storages of CO2, which they still downplay as having fairly small impact... But nobody of them are talking about the reduced levels of Relative Humidity, which not only lead to less precipitation, but also to the drying out of soil, as the dry air is attracting moisture from anywhere it can get its hands on, including from soil. And <u>lower Relative Humidity stops **glaciers and polar caps from growing back too in the same way** – it forces them to dry off...</u> Yes, this is true and very interesting phenomenon! Namely, when the air is very saturated with water, it leads to some of this water freezing on top of glaciers and polar caps. Saturated air loses its water whenever it can, whatever it touches. When the air is dry, the opposite processes start – the air is taking away whatever moisture it can from these glaciers and polar caps and soil and anything, really!. It is, as I once already said, as if the air is thirsty. All that means – the glaciers are losing water not only because they are melting slightly faster, which they are, but also because they are drying out which is caused by a drier air.*

And nobody is bothered. Instead, scientists and media and politicians are frequently talking about dangers that would come if we started to restore forests... Really???!!! Who indeed needs enemies... But that is sooo true! Many scientists and media are indeed spreading the message that Afforestation would be dangerous and bad altogether to our planet. Read the next article for that and keep in mind, that this is only one of such articles in those mainstream media!

BBC's article from 26th May 2020, by Michael Marshal

Planting trees doesn't always help with climate change

<u>Reforestation is seen as a way to help cool the climate, sucking excess warming carbon out of the atmosphere. But it's not always that simple.</u>

Suddenly we are all being told to plant trees. The hope is that they will save us from the worst effects of climate change.

*The idea is everywhere. The Swedish climate activist **Greta Thunberg** has made a film arguing for extra protections for the world's forests, and for the replanting of those that have been cut down. **George Monbiot**, a columnist in the UK's **Guardian** newspaper, has founded a campaign called Natural Climate Solutions, which advocates restoring forests and other ecosystems.*

*This is not just talk. The UK government has planted millions of trees over the last decade and has pledged another million between 2020 and 2024. Others have attempted far more dramatic feats: in 2016 one Indian state planted 50 million trees in one day, while in July last year Ethiopia claimed to have planted 350 million in a day. Even the UK's **Daily Mail**, a right-wing newspaper not known for its climate activism, has just launched a campaign encouraging all its readers to plant a tree.*

Note! – If there is one thing that history has proven, these things cannot be left voluntary to everyone himself. This just doesn't work. After all, the world is losing **280 thousand sq. km** <u>of forests every year</u>. Activities of some individuals or local groups, organizations will change nothing. It is still good, of course, but will change nothing.

The scale needed is completely different now. It must be global and enforced process.

Back to the article!

> *Protecting existing forests and planting new ones are surely good things to do. <u>However, scientists say we must not place too much faith in trees to save us</u>. In particular, last year one research group claimed we can plant a trillion extra trees and* **remove a quarter of the carbon dioxide currently in the air**. *These figures have been widely criticised as overhyped and unreliable. Trees will definitely help us slow climate change, but they won't reverse it on their own.*
>
> *The underlying problem is that our society is releasing greenhouse gases, especially carbon dioxide (CO2), that are warming the Earth's climate to levels we have never experienced before. As a result the great ice sheets are melting, contributing to rising seas, and extreme weather events like hurricanes and droughts are becoming more severe.*

As you can see, BBC and scientists think that planting trees has little to do with climate change. They think forests will only slow it down... For this reason I have to ask the reader this - Are we going to leave this problem to them? I think, that would be suicidal **Do they** even know that each adult tree releases <u>at least **40 tons of water** in air every season?</u> I would be surprised if they knew this and the fact that the Relative Humidity is in a very sad place too. Maybe they would be able to count 2 and 2 together and understand where the 4 comes from, as there is a clear correlation. But I doubt they can figure out the true causes of Climate Change by themselves. Also (again...), CO2 levels have increased by only **one ten thousandths** (**0.04%**), while <u>the world has lost at least **50% and up to 80% of the green mass**</u> of its plants. And the atmosphere has been losing huge amount of water every year because of that, let alone the areas that would make the atmosphere cooler because of shadows created by all those territories of trees and shadows of extra clouds also created by them.

Do you remember what I said previously? - With very careful estimates that annually lost water in atmosphere is as large as the territory of whole Egypt, and it would be 5 kilometres deep. So, I really hope that BBC and scientists will wake up to these facts one day. I hope it won't be too late when they do...

I also found another BBC article, earlier than the previous one, where they published something that suggests they should understand the problems of Deforestation. And yet, nobody ever bothered. Of course, they failed to learn how much water each tree is spraying into atmosphere and how much the atmosphere doesn't receive because of those lost forests. Another thing that nobody addresses is that the moist air itself reduces the strength of Sunrays that reach the Earth. After all, scientists falsely think that water is a greenhouse gas which itself leads to higher temperatures. I already explained how it actually works in this very book, and it rather has the opposite effect. Yet so many things in the following article were spot on that I couldn't leave it out. So, let's take a look at it. And especially pay attention to underlined and bolded words.

BBC's article from 12th September 2019, by Rachel Nuwer

What would happen if all the world's trees disappeared?

As the Amazon fires continue to burn, Rachel Nuwer asks: how dependent are we on the survival of forests?

"Forests are the lifeline of our world," says Meg Lowman, director of the Tree Foundation, a non-profit organisation in Florida that is dedicated to tree research, exploration, and

education. "Without them, we lose extraordinary and essential functions for life on Earth."

Trees' services to this planet range from carbon storage and soil conservation to water cycle regulation. They support natural and human food systems and provide homes for countless species – including us, through building materials. Yet we often treat trees as disposable: as something to be harvested for economic gain or as an inconvenience in the way of human development. Since our species began practicing agriculture around 12,000 years ago, we've **cleared nearly half of the world's estimated 5.8 trillion trees**, according to a 2015 study published in the journal Nature.

Much of the deforestation has happened in recent years. Since the onset of the industrial era, **forests have declined by 32%**. Especially in the tropics, many of the world's remaining **three trillion trees** are falling fast, with about **15 billion cut each year**, the Nature study states. In many places, tree loss is accelerating. In August, the National Institute for Space Research showed an **84% increase in fires** in the Brazilian Amazon rainforest compared to the same period in 2018. Slash-and-burn is also especially on the rise in **Indonesia and Madagascar**.

"Let me just start with how horrible a world without trees would be – they are irreplaceable," says **Isabel Rosa**, a lecturer in environmental data and analysis at **Bangor University** in Wales. "If we get rid of all the trees, we will live [on] a planet that might not actually be able to sustain us anymore."

Note! – It will happen much earlier!!!

For starters, if trees disappeared overnight, so would much of the planet's biodiversity. Habitat loss is already the primary *driver of extinction worldwide, so the destruction of all remaining forests would be "catastrophic" for plants, animals, fungi and more, says Jayme Prevedello, an ecologist at Rio de Janeiro State University in Brazil. "There would be massive extinctions of all groups of organisms, both locally and globally."*

The wave of extinctions would extend beyond forests, depleting wildlife that depends on single trees and small stands of trees as well. In 2018, Prevedello and his colleagues found, for example, that **overall species richness was 50 to 100% higher** *in areas with scattered trees than in open areas. "Even a single, isolated tree in an open area can act as a biodiversity 'magnet,' attracting and providing resources for many animals and plants," Prevedello says. "Therefore, losing even individual trees can severely impact biodiversity locally."*

*The planet's climate would also be drastically altered in the short and long term. <u>Trees mediate the water cycle by acting as biological pumps: they suck water from the soil and deposit it into the atmosphere by transforming it from liquid to vapour.</u> By doing this, <u>forests contribute to</u> **cloud formation** <u>and precipitation</u>. Trees also prevent flooding by trapping water rather than letting it rush into lakes and rivers, and by buffering coastal communities from storm surges. They keep soil in place that would otherwise wash away in rain, and their root structures help microbial communities thrive.*

<u>Without trees, formerly forested areas would become drier and more prone to extreme droughts</u>. When rain did come, flooding would be disastrous. Massive erosion would impact oceans, smothering coral reefs and other marine habitats. Islands stripped of trees would lose their barriers to the ocean, and many would be washed away. "Removing trees means losing

huge amounts of land to the ocean," says **Thomas Crowther**, a global systems ecologist at **ETH Zurich** in Switzerland and lead author of the 2015 Nature study.

In addition to mediating the water cycle, trees have a localised cooling effect. They provide shade that maintains soil temperatures and, as the darkest thing in the landscape, they absorb heat rather than reflect it. In the process of **evapotranspiration**, they also channel energy from solar radiation into converting liquid water into vapour. With all of those cooling services lost, most places where trees formerly stood would immediately become warmer. In another study, Prevedello and his colleagues found that complete removal of a 25 sq. km patch of forest caused **local annual temperatures to increase** by at least 2C in tropical areas and 1C in temperate areas. Researchers have also **found similar temperature differences** when comparing forested and open areas.

End of the article!

As you just read, the only thing they didn't mention here is the effect of trees on Relative Humidity. But that is linked to cloud formation, which they did mention here. Everything else seems to be spot on. Yet, with this article BBC's activities seem to have stopped with respect to this topic. But we don't expect much from them anyway. They are famous for being very unreliable when it comes to all kinds of information...

Now, let us move on to the second task we have to do in order to save our planet.

2. **Drastically reduce the consumption of wood by limiting use of papers, wooden packaging etc.**

We have to reduce the use of wood as much as possible in order to help the woodlands to start the recovery process. That will move us faster to achieving our goal - Afforestation. Things as wooden fences and one-time wooden packaging should disappear from our menu. The consumption of paper should go down dramatically too. Also, we have piles of useless books and magazines, newspapers being printed at incredible volumes daily. People buy them and then throw them out nearly instantly. We don't save paper at all. But all of that is lost woodlands. Also, with growing population numbers and prosperity, the use of paper (loss of woodlands) also increases. All of that should be drastically reduced via government intervention if we want to survive this storm of the collapse of the Ecosystems.

3. **Start reducing numbers of people on this planet by introducing One Child Policy everywhere on the globe till sustainable levels are achieved. Yes, it will lead to older society in general, and the retirement ages will have to be changed significantly too. But the cost of not doing it is much higher and more painful.**

As hard as it sounds to you now, any other solutions will not help if we don't sort out this problem. And each country should be controlling their own numbers. No country that cannot control their numbers should be allowed to use the resources of our planet freely and limitlessly. We either are tough all together, or we all will die all together before suffering enormously, starting with our kids.

The thing is – if there is at least one country that keeps breeding uncontrollably (especially if that is supported by their religion...), they inevitably will run out of resources even for basic things, like arable land etc., as they will annihilate all ecosystems around them. THAT IS

INEVITABLE WITH OVERPOPULATED COUNTRIES. And then they will have no choice but to move to other lands/countries. Most likely, they will move to those neighbouring lands that are less populated. And they will be ready to do anything to get there and take it over, especially if this overpopulated one has much larger numbers. So, in essence, countries that keep breeding uncontrollably become a future danger not only to themselves and environment, but also to their neighbours. Sooner or later they will start do demand resources of all kinds from their neighbours, or their whole society will suffer from starvation due to ruined Natural Cycles. In this case, wars will become inevitable. But what if the whole world is already overpopulated? Where are we going to go then? Then it will simply turn into wars, starvation, and diseases, known as the three horses of the Apocalypse... And we are really closing in towards this scenario.

One such country that will suffer very soon from draughts and overpopulation is Iran.

Wikipedia:

> *Iran's population grew rapidly during the latter half of the 20th century, increasing from about **19 million in 1956** to about **85 million by February 2023**. However, Iran's **fertility rate** has dropped significantly in recent years, coming down from a fertility rate of 6.5 per woman to just a little more than 1.7 two decades later, leading to a population growth rate of about 1.39% as of 2018. Due to its young population, studies project that the growth will continue to slow until it stabilizes around 105 million by 2050.*

Trust me, Iran will never reach 105 million, because the Nature will stop all of us with ecological catastrophe.

Iran's official density is very low. It is only **48 people per sq. km**. However, this country consists mainly of deserts. As you just read, its population grew 4 times between 1956 and 2023... They are experiencing serious problems with the lack of water already now. Yet, their predicted numbers by 2050 is said to be **105 million**... It is known that these deserted countries are heavily using groundwater too. And it is known that this groundwater is disappearing because the overuse of it as it is anywhere in the world. How are they going to feed those 105 million people, if they won't be able even to provide them with water very soon. And it will affect absolutely everyone in their country...

Strangely, one of the most efficient ways to reduce the numbers of people in any given society is by increasing their prosperity. But not simply by giving them money. We should create a system, where decent work will lead to decent prosperity and security of it to anyone who is working hard. Chinas numbers even under One Child policy have been raising rapidly. It stopped only after China had reached certain levels of prosperity. The highest birth numbers are in the poorest countries, like India, Africa, Brazil...Some religions, like Abrahamic Religions, are also a problem, as they keep encouraging their followers to breed as much as they can... This should stop! They put in danger all of us.

Certain prosperity and prospects in life give people some purpose in life and hope for a better future. And they are more in control of their lives, including the fact that they can better control how many kids they will have. Also, they are more conscious about the protection in case they don't want kids, as prosperity comes hand in hand not only with more options, but also with better education levels. People in prosperous societies, if they aren't members of religious sects, know that they will give more to their kids if there will be only one or two of them. On top of that, they will be more productive themselves in their professional lives too. Mothers of large families are too busy and tired from dealing with kids. And they are out of the job market for most of their lives adding to shortages of workers.

Also, the happiest and least corrupt societies are those that have the smallest differences between the top earners and lower earners. And in these countries the prosperity in general tends to be the highest too along with small birth rates which comes as a consequence to all of that. In essence, correct taxation policies lead to reduction of number and wealth levels of super-rich, and it also leads to decent living of the majority and leads to reduced birth-rates. So, yes, in many ways higher taxes to the rich (progressive taxation on all levels) is also a tool to get closer to this goal of reducing global population. And benefits from that don't end there. But that is a story for another time.

One thing that we shouldn't do is to introduce minimum income regardless of whether person contributes to society or not. Not only this will fail to reduce the numbers of population, but it also can lead to some people being encouraged to create large families, as they all will be provided and there is nothing else they might want to do in their lives as they are fully provided.

4. Stop urbanisation and globalization. These lead to longer supply chains and, for that reason, larger consumption.

We are told that globalization has made us all wealthier. This is not completely true. The West has clearly benefitted from that. But that came with many other problems, some of which we already addressed in this book. Urbanization is one of such problems as it leads to extended supply chains. But that leads to larger demand for storages (warehouses), roads, vehicles, and containers for transportation of goods etc. Globalization creates the same problem. There is no reason for cars from Europe being shipped to the USA and the other way around. And the same is true with produce. This so-called business and trade creates additional employment without any other gain but variety of products. But it all leads to way higher consumption rates and not only because of transportation needs.

If we calculated all people involved in this absolutely useless transportation and maintenance of all infrastructure and machines involved in transportation of these goods from one country to another, we could conclude that this has only made the world busier and made us consume more, including in terms of fossil fuels. In short, urbanization and globalization makes us busier and increases energy consumption. It is all concealed behind the claims of providing us with larger numbers of choices, with better standards of life etc... In reality it creates fake employment, waste of resources, increases pollution, makes the super-rich even more rich and leads to a large numbers of people spending their lives at work just to survive from salary to salary. It is the true **RAT RACE**. Whoever is a big fighter against Climate Change and has nothing against these facts and the impact of globalization and urbanization on Climate Change and Deforestation, is wasting their lives barking at the wrong tree.

5. Start to restore the swamps and peatlands.

Peatlands are huge depositaries of the CO_2. But we really need them as fertilizers for the soil too. The only thing that would satisfy both sides was if we created a system in which we helped the Nature to grow them back at a similar rate to how much we use them. After all, we call ourselves intelligent beings... That means, we should understand these things and act accordingly. Namely, we should understand the need to keep the Nature in balance and help it if needed. Up to this day we are only mercilessly taking from it, and our numbers and appetite keeps growing. All of that is beyond sustainable.

I remember how in Soviet times scientists were very proud of their achievements at draining the swamps and making from those areas agricultural lands. In reality, they heavily affected huge areas of these peatlands and swamps, which might have been extremely important part of local ecosystems. We know for sure that this led to near extinction of local **swamp turtles**. I have no clue how they are called in English properly. I translated their names directly from Latvian. Either way, there are huge areas that have been drained. And with Deforestation levels as they are today on top of that, no wonder Latvia has experienced the driest spring in their history. It is so dry, in fact, that it will lead to very severe loss of harvest of all kinds of crops. Also, this is being affected by Deforestation in Russia too. Still, not a single person manages to link these problems with these specific human activities...

Swamps have also increased the numbers of different kinds of flies and mosquitoes. Even though they are annoying to humans, they are also a food for birds. By draining them we affect numbers of all life around us. And yet, we are very proud of that! Why?

6. Drastically reduce the consumption of animal meat.

This might be one of the most important and fastest things at the given moment to achieve. The thing is – if around 70% of all arable land that right now is dedicated to produce meat, and we can live with much less of meat (or simply use only poultry), then we can use it for Afforestation. And that would give us huge territories for woodlands. It would be close to those **20 million sq. km**... After all, if we don't have any other arable land on our planet available for restoration of woodlands, then we have to compromise. As you already know, the only other alternative is – we keep living as we do today till the planet dies. And that might be much sooner than you think. As I said, looking at acceleration of severity and lengths of draughts, and how they affect harvests, it wouldn't surprise me if we only had 5 years left if we don't start right now!

I am sure I have forgotten many important points that would make my arguments even stronger. Yet, I know that here you have read enough to be persuaded that something is terribly wrong. I can only remind you to watch that documentary – **Pumped Dry**!, as there it shows the scale and speed of changes. And that move was made in year **2015**, meaning, 8 years later today things are already worse than they were at the time this movie was made.

JURIS BOGDANOVS

Authors page

We all come from our childhood. We normally don't remember our early years. However, our personalities and our thinking algorithms are formed in those days of our childhood. And it is those specific thinking algorithms that will determine our behaviour and choices in life, including how strong or weak willpower we will have etc. This is why our childhood is very important to understand ourselves.

This is me in my childhood during Soviet Union era in Latvia!

Later in life, based on mental, intellectual, and spiritual things we have received during our childhood, we can either adopt, learn, and stay strong throughout any challenges life gets us into, or we get broken at every test that comes our way.

So, it all starts in childhood. I can only wish that we, as humans, realised how important are spiritual, intellectual, and cultural things we go through in childhood and create environments where every child receives things that would make them strong and happy and good humans. Without the knowledge about what it is, how it works and how to organize our lives in order to achieve the best results we cannot achieve much as a society. We are deeply connected to the broader society surrounding us. The society, and socially economic environment in it, forms us into what we become. In short, we reflect the society or failures of society in which we grew up. Later we ourselves become the ones who create the environment around us and add to formation of the next generations. We make them in our spiritual image in the same way as the previous generations have made us in theirs. And keep in mind that we affect and are affected not only by our direct family, but also by everyone we meet in our lives. That means, we have to care about all of our neighbours (neighbouring nations...) and their wellbeing too if we want to live in a happy world. And we have to respect and listen to each other. Not doing anything bad to our neighbours isn't enough. After all, not helping somebody who needs help might also turn out to be a crime in certain situations. And the consequences that might emerge from this ignorance of the troubles of our neighbours might hit us ourselves many years later. WE ARE ALL CONNECTED IN MANY WAYS!

What we become reflects whatever has been surrounding us in our early days. Our choices in life are fairly determined by that environment. The languages we speak is only one of such expressions. I call it the Law of Reflection! The Law of Reflection works on absolutely all levels. Only that it doesn't work instantly like with reflections of our images in mirror. This reflection works more like Chicken-and-Egg reflection. This means, chicken can only reproduce other chickens, and nothing else. First there will be eggs, then they will turn into chickens that will be laying eggs again, and the cycle goes on and on. There will never emerge a fish from the egg of the chicken.

And the same is true on spiritually intellectual level. We reflect the society that we were surrounded with when we grew up, and we will recreate the same values in the next generation by simply being part of the social life in it. All successes in the given society will be also our successes, as will be its failures. Many things still can be changed later in life, if we understand how things work and why we are what we are. Namely, we can create the information environment that would elaborate in us those views and strengths that we wish to improve. Of course, it would require some planning and work to achieve those changes, but we can change nearly everything. We simply have to start with understanding ourselves and the role of intellectual environment around of us.

This is me now! Making my living somewhere in England...

I grew up in Soviet Union. We lived in a very remote place and didn't socialise much. We were poor. Looking at technologies of the current world it never stops amazing me. Sometimes I feel like a man from the stone age who was given all of these devices and everything. We didn't even have a landline telephone in house. We had to go to our neighbours if we needed to call somebody. A simple radio and TV (black and white, smallish) were our only technologies. We didn't have a water and toilet inside of the house. We also didn't have a fridge for the large part of my childhood. And the TV only had few programs that only run at certain times of the day. If I told you that I even had to do ploughing with a horse in my teens, would you believe it? So yes, for that reason, I really appreciate all things that we all have today, and I am constantly amazed by them. They still feel like incredible miracles to me every day.

Having said that, I remember my childhood in very bright colours. It is true that happiness isn't in number of things you own. You truly might own nothing and be happy. Unfortunately, that shouldn't be a condition for being happy either, as some extremely wealthy people nowadays want to make us believe and push us into, while remaining extremely wealthy themselves...

In our family nobody was telling me anything about religion, politics, technologies, sciences, anything really... And I didn't bother much with anything of that myself. At least it seemed so. However, quite early in my life I realised that when I came across certain views or behaviour patterns of humans (individuals) I was questioning them. And I did it not for the sake of questioning, but because I wanted to understand why things are happening as they are, why people behave or think in a certain way, and why different people do it so very differently.

Very often I came across situations where several people had several opinions about the same problem or situation. And it wasn't about them trying to figure out something that isn't really clear, but it was conclusions about what comes from what, what are the right solutions etc. I always felt that there should be an ultimate answer that resolves everything absolutely perfectly and which has been based on considering all the involved facts with respect to this problem. But absolutely always I didn't have a clue about what those facts and what those answers were. At the same time I also always promised to myself that I will keep looking for understanding and answers in order to figure everything out everything by myself, to understand why different people believe in different things and behave so differently, and most importantly, what could be the single perfect answer to the question at hand.

The funny thing is, I have had a fairly bad memory, especially with names my whole life. I never liked remembering places and dates and names. It bored me. I liked to understand the substance of things and processes leading to certain situations, if I could, but not to learn things that were told to me by somebody else. This is why I wasn't shining in science classes at all. Of course, some claims in Quantum Mechanics made my brain jump. However, later in life I realised that those claims might be insane interpretations of reality which have nothing to do with what is actually happening.

I remember few stories from my childhood that would sum up how I felt. On one occasion, when I just started school, it must have been at the age of 7 or so, the teacher asked the class to look at the back wall of the classroom. There was a portrait of a fairly bald man with a beard. She said that this is a very remarkable man. His name is **Vladimir Ilyich Lenin**, and he is our **leader**. Before this occasion I have never heard the word "leader". Teacher tried to explain something about it to us, but I didn't get it anyway. And if honestly, I didn't care at that age at all, nor did I at any age after that even though the name of this person kept coming up again and again and again till we all knew it even if woken in the middle of night.

In those Soviet times we had to listen to propaganda all the time. Nothing of that was interesting or relevant to me even when I was 16 years old. In fact, famous people aren't relevant to me even now. And it was the same with everything around me. Everything about politics felt nearly alien and not related to my life at all. I couldn't learn anything of that because it felt irrelevant, alien to me.

On another occasion, when I could have been around 10 years old or so, the teacher for some reason was talking about the God. Would you trust me if I told you that I had no clue what it is at this age? Well, I didn't. The teacher told us that some time ago humans were not so bright and believed in some mythical (another concept I was struggling with) beings, where one of them was God. I started to question this teacher about this God, as I really wanted to know their arguments for why they believed in this God. Maybe there is a good reason to believe in it after all! But the teacher got annoyed by that and simply shut me up saying that it isn't true anyway, and I simply have to accept it. And at that moment I promised to myself that when I will grow up, or when I find a good source of information, I will definitely find out everything about this God and what arguments led people to believe in it all by myself. This is the first time that I remember myself thinking in this way. Pretty much the same was with many other questions later in my life.

The thing is - my interest in finding out how things work nearly always followed the same pattern. I decided to keep gathering facts and arguments always from all directions (points of view) and grow my own understanding of the topics in question as much as I can. In many ways that became a lifelong obsession in many areas of knowledge. I even realised that it can be compared with being, as if, pregnant with a certain idea, and it keeps growing in you. It keeps growing and developing, and at some point, sometimes after many decades, it results in a birth of a completely formed solution or explanation of certain processes. In this process some premature ideas got out and died as they still haven't reached the needed maturity for surviving...

Slowly many things started to become clearer and clearer. Other things, however, like some theories of science, started to show more and more problems and contradictions. In these cases I said to people that these ideas do not make any sense. And they always replied that I simply haven't read enough books about them and that I don't understand them. In reality, I understood the given stories well enough to see their total failures. They simply had absurd and demonstrably wrong claims in them, which created new questions and had many gaps in the narratives. So, I wasn't ready to accept them purely because somebody with two PhDs and several written books said it is true.

It was never good for me to learn things by heart. This is why I really liked Richard Feynman. He described how the right attitude towards science should be and this was exactly how I felt about it. And he said approximately this – different things have different names in different languages. Knowing all of those names doesn't bring you any closer to understanding of what those things are and how those processes work.

Unfortunately, pretty much the same is true with me reading claims of science. I can read them, I can even remember them, and I definitely know what science books wanted to say with those claims. However, more often than not many of those claims not only don't make any logical sense, but they also appear to be absurd at times. When I say that to scientists, they would never ask me for arguments or facts. They will simply declare that I didn't get the ideas and have to keep reading those books. But those books are simply full of hollow declarations, ignored and misinterpreted results of observations. One such hollow/asserted declaration supports/explains the other. And many of them emerged as assumptions (hypotheses) to start with! So, what is the point to learn their names and their claims? It doesn't bring me any closer to my personal and full understanding of those processes. Yes, it gives me the understanding of what science community thinks about those processes. But that doesn't necessary mean that those are complete or even true depictions of reality. The fact that science community believes in something shouldn't be a proof for anything in its own right. But in current world it is being sold as such. Once again, this is how "**Emperor's New Cloth**" is being sold, and not how science should work.

So, if some claims in science didn't make sense and science was unable and unwilling to address those gaps in their tales, then I simply didn't accept them by openly stating that and challenging science community. Clearly, science community doesn't take that easy. They declare you a crackpot for doing that. And they have no problem calling you names and completely leaving out all the arguments you would bring up. This is why I previously said that contemporary science is in a very, very sad place.

I have no formal education in science. Having said that, I have no formal education in English too. As I said at the beginning of this book, I started to learn English when I already was 33 years old from audiobooks. Later I attended few courses in the UK, but only to gain some papers that would confirm that I can understand some English. And here we are! I am writing a book in English all by myself. Of course, I have no illusions about my grammar, but still... Would you say that I don't know English because I have no formal education and have some problems with grammar? If no, then why would anyone say that I have no knowledge about claims of science and nature of things if I have no formal education in physics?

As I said, I love to understand things, and I keep searching for ultimate answers. The secret is -never settle on anything..., keep the door open...

I studied economics but I also always loved psychology. I wanted to understand human beings and myself so badly ever since I remember myself. I wanted to understand them (and myself) and how the world works around me not by what other people think about all of that, but all by myself... All things simply had to make sense to me, and no gaps were allowed. Whenever there were gaps in any claims of science (sometimes called paradoxes), it would instantly lead to me questioning the whole narrative surrounding the given topic. This approach contaminated all other areas of human activities which I came across. So, I wanted to understand everything and fully...

Studying economics was an accident. It happened simply because at the given moment in my life it was the only thing I could get into. But it proved to be very useful in understanding many processes in politics and human society, and even how those processes affect the psychology of individuals and groups. But physics is just another field which is simply extremely interesting.

I believe that we live in times when many of existing beliefs (scientific beliefs...) will be overturned and this will give us, the humans, a chance to build a great and lasting future for our descendants. This future will be based on new discoveries and understanding in physics. Yes, I feel that another Golden Age for science is just around the corner. And most of the existing ideas in Theoretical Physics will not be part of that.

It was Richard Feynman and Einstein himself who said something that can be interpreted as a claim that understanding is the key, while knowing actual facts for the sake of knowing them is worth little. Namely, if you cannot explain your ideas to a child so that they can fully understand them (don't confuse that with "accept them"), then you don't understand them yourself. And providing piles of hollow declarations ISN'T THE SAME AS EXPLAINING THINGS... I am 100% behind this.

Yet, this world is ruled by people who believe in the opposite of what I just said on all levels. We have many beliefs in physics and economics and psychology, let alone religion, which are mere wishful thinking.

Abrahamic Religions, for instance, have proved that they are filled with nonsense and hatred and whitewashing of their own blunders, which are too numerous to be counted. These religions have contaminated (poisoned???) with the same insanity everything around us, including sciences. I call this phenomenon, which they created - "**The Art of Interpretation**". And I mean it in a bad sense. This is bad when you ignore clear facts and keep pretending that true facts are those assumptions of yours which you want to be true contrary to reality. So, you end up simply running around in circles and doing your absolutely best to reach the only conclusions YOU WAANT TO BE TRUE instead of facing the Truth! AND NOBODY EVEN KNOWS WHAT THIS CONCEPT "TRUTH" ACTUALLY MEAN... I do! But that is a topic for another book... In short, delusion and self-deceit is the middle name of our times. And it is exactly the same with our sciences too. By the way, it has been the failures of science that paved the way to the Movement of Flat Earth Theory. This is why I will be addressing this topic in one of mine future books too. Trust me, it is a fascinating topic...

JURIS BOGDANOVS

THIS AND THAT

I recently came across an article addressing the question about why scientists refuse alternative ideas. It is an interesting read and sounds very genuine. Here is the article:

https://bigthink.com/starts-with-a-bang/scientists-hostile-new-ideas/

The good reasons scientists are so hostile to new ideas

KEY TAKEAWAYS

Many people, including both laypersons and scientists, often have wild, revolutionary ideas that would overturn much of what is presently known and accepted by science. However, these ideas rarely gain traction, and are quick to be shot down by many within the relevant scientific field. Although it often appears that science, and scientists, are cruel and hostile to new ideas, this is actually a hallmark of being sceptical and scrupulous.

In my experience, science community not only never looks at those new facts and arguments, and ignore facts that prove their ideas wrong altogether, but they literally turn around and stop talking if anyone would even mention that most of currently accepted ideas are wrong and there are solid facts proving alternative ideas. In my experience there is absolutely nothing that can be called scrupulous. It is more like religious zeal to protect the existing ideas. But let's continue reading that article.

(By Ethan Siegel)

Every few months, a novel headline will fly across the world, claiming to revolutionize one or more of our most deeply held scientific ideas. The declarations are always sweeping and revolutionary, ranging from "The Big Bang never happened" to "This idea does away with dark matter and dark energy" to "Black holes aren't real" to "Maybe this unexpected astronomical phenomenon is due to aliens." And yet, despite the glowing coverage of the novel proposal, it most frequently languishes in obscurity, attracting little mainstream attention other than a myriad of dismissals.

Commonly, it's portrayed that scientists in this particular field are dogmatic, wedded to old ideas, and close-minded. This narrative might be popular among contrarian scientists or those who themselves hold fringe beliefs, but it paints a disingenuous picture of the scientific truth. In reality, the evidence supporting the prevailing theories are overwhelming, and the new headline-grabbing proposals are no more compelling than the scientist's equivalent of playing in the sandbox.

Every few months, a novel headline will fly across the world, claiming to revolutionize one or more of our most deeply held scientific ideas. The declarations are always sweeping and revolutionary, ranging from "The Big Bang never happened" to "This idea does away with dark matter and dark energy" to "Black holes aren't real" to "Maybe this unexpected astronomical phenomenon is due to aliens." And yet, despite the glowing coverage of the novel proposal, it most frequently languishes in obscurity, attracting little mainstream attention other than a myriad of dismissals.

Commonly, it's portrayed that scientists in this particular field are dogmatic, wedded to old ideas, and close-minded. This narrative might be popular among contrarian scientists or those who themselves hold fringe beliefs, but it paints a disingenuous picture of the scientific truth. In reality, the evidence supporting the prevailing theories are overwhelming, and the new headline-grabbing proposals are no more compelling than the scientist's equivalent of playing in the sandbox. Here are the four big flaws that commonly occur with new ideas, and why you'll never hear about most of them again after they're first put forth.

Our Universe, from the hot Big Bang until the present day, underwent a huge amount of growth and evolution, and continues to do so. Although we have a large amount of evidence for dark matter, it doesn't really make its presence known until many years have passed since the Big Bang, which means that dark matter may have been created at that time or earlier, with many scenarios remaining viable.

(Credit: NASA/CXC/M. Weiss)

1.) When you work, every day, with "the real McCoy," you can immediately spot an impostor's shortcomings. In science, we have accumulated an enormous body of knowledge — a set of experimental and observational data — and a set of theories that provides a framework to accurately describe the governing rules of our reality. Many of the results that we obtained were initially bizarre and counterintuitive, with multiple theoretical possibilities proposed to explain them. Over time, further experiments and observations winnowed them down, and the most successful theories with the greatest degrees of validity were the ones that survived.

Proposals that attempt to revolutionize one (or more) of our accepted theories have a large suite of hurdles to overcome. In particular, they must:

- reproduce all the successes of the prevailing theory,
- explain a phenomenon more successfully than the current theory can,
- and make novel predictions that can be tested that differ from the theory it's attempting to supersede.

It's very rare that all three of these criteria are met. In fact, the overwhelming majority of these grand proposals fail on even the first point.

The interesting thing about this site was that I have sent several of my works (with facts and arguments) to them too. Of course, I cannot be sure that they have read anything of that, as many people in science community instantly throw out anything that challenges them.

Clearly, if science works like Mr Siegel says it does, it should be very legitimate, solid, and credible way indeed to do science. In reality, though, most of officially accepted ideas in Theoretical Physics have enormous gaps and completely wrong claims in them. The fact that you haven't heard about most of them only proves that science community isn't willing to address them at all. Also, to keep their so-called vetted and verified theories alive, like about the true pattern of Magnetic Field, Gravity, Gravitational Lensing, what is Vacuum etc, they have decided to ignore large number of facts clearly proving (not even hinting) that these currently accepted theories are plain wrong. Some of those facts I already mentioned (about Gravity, Gravitational Lensing, and Vacuum) in this book. Many others are in other books.

There is a very interesting thing about the so-called social platforms such as YouTube, Facebook, Quora.com and others when it comes to questioning science. They have their like and dislike buttons. But those buttons aren't there only for statistics. If some ideas receive a lot of dislikes, let alone they are reported as not scientific or something, the algorithms of these platforms would instantly stop suggesting anything you post there to others. I have an account on **Quora.com**. It is here:

https://**www.quora.com**/profile/Juris-Bogdanovs-1

This site is about questions and answers on whatever topic you like. As if... Anyone can contribute, no matter what the question is. In my experience, it has been infested with science hardliners, who religiously push forward the existing theories and do their best to block anything that contradicts their pre-existing beliefs. And with that approach no new ideas would get far because the dislikes will kill them.

Interestingly, I have provided a lot of evidence for certain topics in certain articles, and yet, not a single one of them was ever properly addressed. The best you can get from science community is those "**Emperor's New Cloth questions**", such as – Do you have a PhD to write anything of that?, or this one - How comes the whole science community around the world sticks with the existing theories but you, not officially trained in science, dare to declare that you have spotted serious faults in the existing theories and figured out how things might actually work? And this is where any discussions end, as they also downvote your articles.

All in all, nobody is interested in facts despite science community endlessly repeating that they only rely on facts and facts alone. All they do is pull out their "**Emperor's New Cloth slogans**" and attack you with them, label your posts as pseudo-scientific and, in this way, prevent them from being shown to anybody else. Their main moto is – facts are irrelevant when it comes to questioning the Holy, Sacred, Supreme theories of the self-appointed all-knowing and never-being-wrong geniuses of science. They loath facts that prove them wrong.

For instance, I have written an article about the Magnetic Field with several solid facts explained in it. It is here:

https://thesciencespace.quora.com/I-have-written-and-sent-to-several-science-journals-my-findings-interpretation-and-proof-about-the-possible-true-Patter

I posted it in the group called **The Science Space.** This group is all about science. Before that some of my articles were blocked by this group. I asked moderators to explain themselves, and one of them said that I should send my materials to him, and he would publish them. So, I did, and it was published. It seemed to gather views quickly, but very quickly stopped. It was all due to religious group called "the true science community" who blocked my article. Possibly, they even sent some bad feedback to moderators, as later I tried to post some other interesting facts from the realm of Theoretical Physics, and they never replied to nor published anything from me again after that...

Let's take a look again at what Mr Siegel wrote:

> *Many of the results that we obtained were initially bizarre and counterintuitive, with multiple theoretical possibilities proposed to explain them. Over time, further experiments and observations winnowed them down, and the most successful theories with the greatest degrees of validity were the ones that survived.*

As I said, the so-called "most successful theories" are only successful if science community ignores facts which prove them completely wrong. For that reason, the article Mr Siegel has written isn't worth the paper it was put on. And I have no problem with "**initially bizarre and counterintuitive results**". What I have problem with is BIZARRE AND COUNTERINTUITIVE INTERPRETATIONS OF WHAT IS ACTUALLY HAPPENING. That is the true pseudo-science.

Of course, we must thank **Abrahamic Religions** for that twisted approach as it is they with who it all started and now they have poisoned the whole world with what I call "**the Art of Interpretation**". This happens when there is an obsessive desire for certain communities to present reality in certain way. Then they don't even realize how they are seeing the desired results and confirmations in absolutely everything. It is known as CONFIRMATIONAL BIAS... But in this case, it has become like an obsession that has blinded the minds of science community all around the world. Our world is literally littered with this approach on all levels, including politics, medicine, and science. This is like a curse that covers the whole world from sea to sea... And the recent events that lasted for two years, medicine wise..., (from start of 2020 to the end of 2021) only confirm that.

On top of that ask yourself this - **Why is science community so resistant to carrying out the experiment I am proposing in order to test the true essence of Vacuum in Space? After all, it is so simple and cheap to do. It doesn't add anything to the cost of any Space mission. And my predictions from this experiment are completely opposite to what science expects from it as I have described it in this book previously.**

Science community cannot simply come out and say that any alternative theories are wrong simply because they have a very strong arguments (more like creeds...) for the existing ones. This is not a scientific approach. This is more like "**Emperor's New Cloth excuse**" for not looking at facts. After all, I AM exposing facts that prove the number and size of the problems with the existing theories, and I AM providing testable suggestions with facts which are already confirming these alternative theories. So, what stops science community from looking at those facts and carrying out those experiments? Ignorance? Arrogance? Lack of scientific spirit? Take your pick! And Mr Siegel is wrong about how science works in the realm of Theoretical Physics.

Think of it - such ideas as **Dark Matter** and **Dark Energy**, for instance, aren't even being questioned by science community. Both these things have qualities and properties that are typical to things that don't exist at all in the same way as does the current understanding of what is Vacuum. Also, these phenomena, if they existed, create absurd situations which appear to be beyond anything that could have any logical explanation, like what is pulling everything in the Universe apart and how abnormally huge that force must be...

Scientists will tell you that these phenomena are real because they have been observed. So, the data confirm them, right? And you cannot even argue with those facts. Or can you? The thing is – those observations are true, and it seems that how could anyone question the existence of these "dark things" if there are all these facts, right?

In reality, both these claims about these "dark things" emerged as a result of faulty other theories before them and on which these two are based. I already told you how the existing theories of Einstein about Gravity (and Gravitational Lensing) are extremely faulty and based on ignorance of very important failures of them and other facts that are pushed aside and ignored. So, the idea of the Dark Matter is a result of these faulty ideas of Einstein. Similarly it goes with the Dark Energy too. It is based on assumption about how Light works and what it is made of. But the existing ideas about Light came as a result from another faulty assumption – the claim that Vacuum is substances free areas.... So, Light lost its medium. And this is where everything turned mysterious... What is Light then, if it propagates without any medium? And the claim that the Speed of Light is constant (absolute) added another absurdity to the tale. IT HAS NEVER BEEN PROVEN TO BE TRUE, BY THE WAY... For more information on this topic check my book – "**about the heavily misinterpreted NATURE OF LIGHT, REDSHIFT and DARK ENERGY**".

If you remember, I already explained how absurd this claim about matter free Vacuum is. It is the same as when declaring that Vacuum consists of something that physically doesn't exist. So, does it exist at all in such a way? Only my experiment could tell that! If proven that Vacuum still is fully filled with some kind of substance, the Light would regain its medium as would Magnetism and Gravity.

As you can see, my proposals fully fit into what Mr Siegel expects from any new theory to be even considered. They can (especially my proposals for the true pattern of Magnetic Field and the true essence of Vacuum) fully reproduce the success of the prevailing theories. More about Vacuum in my book – "**The True Essence of Vacuum**".

My proposals also explain the given phenomena more successfully than the current ideas. And most importantly, they have predictions from the results of some experiments that would overturn the existing theories. The problem is though – nobody in science community is ever going to look into anything of that, let alone do those experiments. They simply don't want to do that for the sake of protecting the existing theories, on which they have been working for their whole lives and from researching which they have been earning their science degrees, their living etc. It is similar to when British Empire was collapsing. Nobody wanted to admit it. Nobody wanted to allow it. But whatever phenomenon has reached the end of its life, and whatever the reason for that end is, it has to go and disappear. To try to stop it is like trying to stop an avalanche with your bare hands. We have to let to die things that have reached the end and burry them. And the end of the current ideas in Theoretical Physics has come. They will be replaced and abandoned because they have no leg to stand on. After all, the Big Bang theory is so wrong that calling it a pseudoscientific theory is like a compliment to its creators.

So, I hope you enjoyed reading this book and you became at least slightly more open minded. If you have got this far with this book, it means that your mind is more opened compared to most people in science community already anyway. Anyway, I hope that you found at least something to take away from this book...

About other books of mine...

For those of you who had the patience to read through the whole book, I have prepared a short description of the content of my other books. Some of them are already ready, some others are still on the way. Please, see the following pages for this.

Next is the list of those books that are already published and some of others that are still on their way:

1. **The True Essence of Vacuum.**

2. **about the heavily misinterpreted NATURE OF LIGHT, REDSHIFT and DARK ENERGY**

3. **The True Distances to Stars and the Size of the Universe.**

4. **How MAGNETISM, TIDES and GRAVITY Actually Work.**

5. **The Mystery of Gravitational Attraction.**

6. **Where Do the UNIVERSE and LIFE Come From.**

7. **HOLLOW EARTH THEORY versus FLAT EARTH THEORY.** (on the way)

8. **The Glory and Curse of Abrahamic Religions.** on the way)

First book: **"The True Essence of Vacuum"** (ready)

As the title suggests, this book is dedicated to the True Essence of Vacuum. And yes, this topic is also in the other book. However, here are more details about the whole story. In this book I am trying to explain and prove that a Matter-free Space is impossible and how to prove by testing that any Space is always fully filled with a substance which Particles are always in full contact with each other and all other objects around them if they are in touch with them. In this book I am suggesting experiments and predict results from them which are only possible if my hypothesis is correct. Also, I will show and explain there some smaller experiments that already have proved my hypothesis. On top of that, as a bonus, in this book I address and explain the blunders of **Time Dilation**. *Trust me – after having brought this one up to your science teacher, your will put him/her in a very difficult situation, as science has no answers to these arguments. So, feel free to challenge your science teachers with everything you can! Wink!*

Second book: "**about the heavily misinterpreted NATURE OF LIGHT, REDSHIFT and DARK ENERGY**" (ready)

*Clearly, this book addresses another of the most central questions in **Cosmology** – **Redshift**. There is a very huge misunderstanding about it, which derives directly from another misunderstood and misinterpreted hypothesis that was turned into accepted theory for no scientific reason – the **Doppler's Shift**.*

*Yes, Doppler's Shift is still a hypothesis, as it has never been reliably tested. In this book I am showing and proving that science teachers are literally lying to us when presenting the story of this effect as reliably proven fact. Nothing of it is even remotely true. And the same is true with Redshift... From what we believe about the nature of Redshift, many other wrong ideas emerged. The most famous of them is the **Big Bang theory** and the idea about the mysterious **Dark Energy** that is said to be pulling the whole Universe in all directions. Once again, nothing of that is true and I am proving this is this book. Again, if you want to challenge your science teachers, this book is for you.*

*Also, in this book I explain why **Einstein's idea about Gravity is absurd** and it can only work if there is another Force of Attraction (Gravity) that would make it possible. But since Einstein did not provide any such force or even a hypothesis for it, then his theory cannot explain the effect known as the Gravity and, for this reason, it is useless. So, as you can see, another great opportunity to challenge your science teachers.*

*The last topic of this book is the **Truth about the Speed of Light**. As it turns out, this is another of Einstein's blunders which nobody is brave enough to challenge. The thing is - Einstein declared that the Speed of Light is Absolute. But that leads to absurd and mathematically impossible situations,* which I fully describe in this book. And, of course, I will fully explain what the Speed of Light is constant to and how to experimentally test it. The absurdity of the Absoluteness of the Speed of Light is equally absurd and yet accepted without any scrutiny whatsoever as is **Time Dilation**. This trend of not adhering to the scientific method when accepting these theories should have ended at some point but it just keeps going on and on unchallenged... Where are all those true scientists and science teachers, one might ask...

Third book: **"The True Distances to Stars and the Size of the Universe"** (Ready)

As it turns out, the Distances to Stars as they are suggested by contemporary science are insanely false. They are literally from a few thousand to few hundreds of thousands shorter than science suggest them. To explain and prove that I will fully explain to the reader **the Law of Distance/Size Correlation**. This is very important question as the Distances that are suggested by science currently forbid us even to dream about ever reaching any other Star. I will prove how incredibly unreliable are claims of science and methods used to determine these Distances compared to observable facts. Here I will also explain why the closest Stars should be only half a Light Day away from our Sun. The known Laws of Physics simply don't allow those Distances to be larger. With all that in mind, the whole size of our Galaxy can be only 0.3 to one Light Year across.

So, things that are looked at in this book are these: 1) the Law of Distance/Size Correlation, 2) unreliability of methods used in figuring out the Distances to and Sizes of Stars. Trust me, this is another topic that your science teachers will not be happy to hear... Wink!

Fourth book: **"How MAGNETISM, TIDES and GRAVITY Actually Work"** (ready)

Magnetism and Gravity have been partly addressed in some other of my books already. After all, the True Pattern of Magnetic Field has been published already in the first book on this list along with some descriptions explaining how and what Magnetism and Gravity have in common. However, in all other books this topic has been addressed only partly, especially Gravity. In this book both will be explained fully. And yes, I know why and how Magnetism and Gravity work. I will explain here all observational facts concerning them both and everything will make perfect sense.

Fifth book: **"The Mystery of Gravitational Attraction"** (Ready)

In this book I propose a hypothesis which would explain all observations with respect to the so-called Gravity or Gravitational Attraction. Also, in this book I propose some experiments that would help to test my hypothesis. Along with Gravity, I address here the main problems with Vacuum, as that is a very important part in understanding the Gravitational Attraction, and why, and how the planes fly! Turns out there is a small mystery still that can only be explained if my hypothesis is correct.

<u>Sixth book</u>: **Where Does the UNIVERSE and LIFE Come From.** (ready)

For those of you who expect me to confirm that the theory of Evolution is true and explains the Emergence of Life this book will be a great disappointment. As it turns out, there is virtually not a single proof confirming that this has ever happened or is even possible.

Yes, species appear to be more advanced from one type of them to another and AS IF DERIVING FROM EACH OTHER. However, this fact alone doesn't mean that they have evolved naturally and by themselves. If this fact alone proved anything, then somebody in the future could say that our cars also have evolved all by themselves from simple models to more advanced ones instead of being created more advanced by intelligent beings... The fact that we have no clue how to do that with biological species and whether that is possible at all cannot be used to prove that it isn't. So, instead we can use quite a few hints from ancient legends, including Biblical narrative, that also talk about the origins of Life on Earth. And no, it has absolutely nothing to do with God-Creator, who's existence is more than unlikely to start with and is nowhere found in the Bible. The most likely theory for the emergence of life is very straightforward and amazing. In short, we have been lying to ourselves about many things of our past and were ignorant of facts that are happening all around us.

Seventh book: **"HOLLOW EARTH THEORY and GRAVITY Explained as Never Before"** (on the way)

This probably is the most controversial book of all. However, despite what the title suggests, I don't have an active claim that the Earth is hollow. In this book I will only lead you through all the facts which show that the Hollow Earth idea is possible in principle as the Laws of Physics allow for it. Also, I will quote and discuss the most famous testimonies of some people who claim to have visited this Inner World. And those testimonies are truly amazing.

*Among other things, I will explain (including with results of some experiments that hint that my hypothesis might be correct) that the **Gravity** would work on the inner side of such surface of Hollow Earth as perfectly as it does on the outer side of it. To do that, I will explain the mechanisms behind the Attraction Force which we presently call **Gravity**. However, I will not explain everything with regard to Gravity as this topic is reserved for another book that is on its way already.*

As it turns out, the Hollow Earth (hollow all Cosmic Objects) idea would much better explain the rotational movement of it and of all of them as that would provide a friction-free interaction between different parts of any given Cosmic Object. This idea comes from a hypothesis that rotations are created by the Magnetic Field of the given object. And the Magnetic Field itself is created by some inner mechanisms inside of them. This mechanism is known in science as the Dynamo Effect. More about all of that inside the book.

Trust me, the hypothesis about how Gravity works is really fascinating...

<u>Eighth book</u>: **"Flat Earth Theory in the Light of True Facts"** (On the way)

> *This book sounds like a book for fun rather than science. However, not everything is so simple. In this book I am going to explain why believers in Flat Earth theory are right to question the existing claims of science. And, of course, I will look at yet other facts that science has misinterpreted or which they haven't even addressed, and which directly led to some people starting to ask questions. Since many of those questions have never been reliably answered, some minds started to lean towards the Flat Earth theory.*
>
> *Of course, the Flat Earth idea is absurd and impossible. However, observational facts must be explained. This Flat Earth movement started with the problems of Curvature. Namely, what we should and what we shouldn't see over certain distances if the given curvature is true. and since we see much more than should be possible, there should be some Laws of Physics that explain everything simply and clearly and can be tested experimentally. As it turns out, all of that is possible. Trust me, this topic turned out to be as interesting to explore as it is to learn something new about the reality around us and how science itself has failed us with it.*

<u>This book sounds like a book for fun rather than science. However, not everything is so simple. In this book I am going to explain why believers in Flat Earth theory are right to</u>

Ninth book: **"The Glory and Curse of Abrahamic Religions"** (On the way)

> *Abrahamic Religions have shaped today's world, and they are incredible source of misinterpretations and blunders. Looking at them was a true joy!*

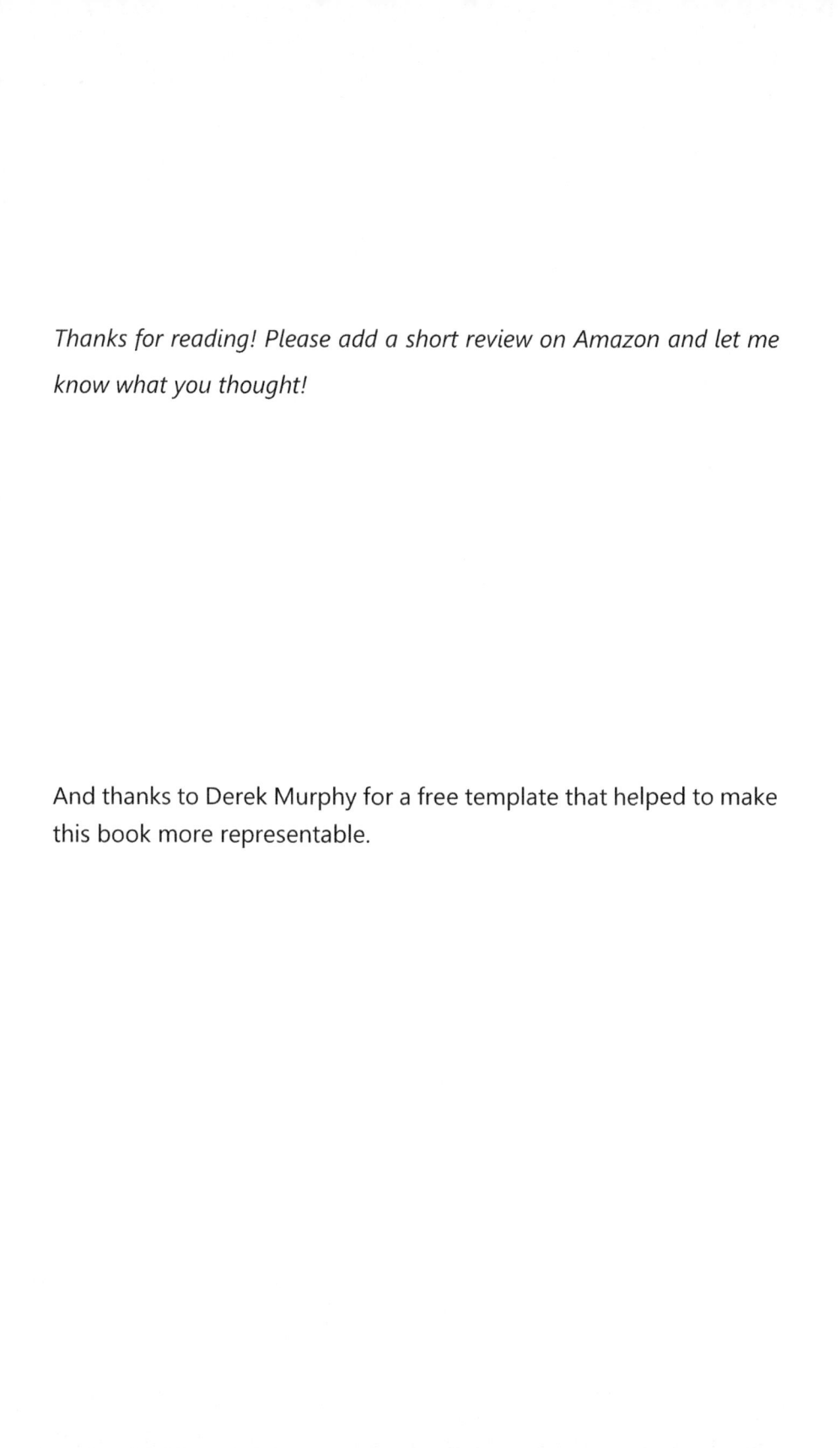

Thanks for reading! Please add a short review on Amazon and let me know what you thought!

And thanks to Derek Murphy for a free template that helped to make this book more representable.

Printed in Great Britain
by Amazon

The Best of Both Worlds

Managing Life with Autism

By Dylan Brown

Copyright © 2022

Dylan Brown

Table Of Content

Who Am I 4
Autism 5
Diagnosis 8
It's Raining Cats and Dogs 11
Communication 14
Education 18
Sensory needs (Hypersensitivity) 22
Special Interests (Obsessions) 26
Literal Dictionary 28
My Story 61
Education: School 62
Weight Loss and Boxing 67
Education: College 69
Relationships 71
Work 73
The Ending 77

Who Am I

My name is Dylan Brown. I am currently 21 years old. I work supporting adults with autism in a residential care setting. I have been doing this for 3 years. It is unusual to see a male working in this type of job, but for me working with autistic people is a passion. I was diagnosed wIth autism (Asperger's) at the age of 12, which has had a big impact on the reason for my job to this day.

Throughout this book, I will give you information about autism and my personal experiences, and my personal knowledge of autism. My main reason for writing this book is that people didn't understand me as a child, and sometimes even now. I was seen as the naughty child or a cheeky chap, but today, I am hoping I can show you my side of the story.

Autism

Autism is not an illness. It does not mean you have a disease. It's just that your brain works a different way from other people.

If you are autistic it doesn't disappear it stays with you for your whole lif e you are born with it or appears at early stages of your life for example when I was very young I was in an out of hospital due to issues with my lungs through out of primary school (elementary) I had been going through some tough stages in year 3 where people around belived me as behaving badly or unusual in year 3 I had a change of teachers 3 times it was hard for me to understand the change of the f irst teacher people with autism sometimes don't cope with change very well and Ofcourse it affected me when the 2nd teacher come along it took me a while to get used to the change and I happend to have a good connection with this teacher I use to have a habit of drawing in the corner of my book and made my work look scruffy I allways believe this teacher knew they was some kind of autism there she come up with the idea of a small piece of paper stuck onto my desk and said to me "draw on this instead of your book" everyday I walked into a school they would be a brand new peice of paper and I never drew in my book again and everything she did within the classroom worked well around then a few months later they was another teacher change without any notice and become more anxiety and challenging behaviour.

Sometimes anxiety can be challenging with notice and letting the person with autism know about the change beforehand.

Being autistic does not stop you from having a good life. Just like everyone else, people with autism have things they are good at as well as things they may struggle with. For example, I am good at doing jigsaws, sports, and games, but I am not so good at communicating, being in a room with lots of people, and sometimes making eye contact. However, being autistic does not mean you can never make friends, have relationships, or get a job. Sometimes you may need extra help with things like this. Let me tell you, I am autistic, and I am 21 years old. I have friends, and I have a fantastic relationship with a partner who understands me. We are getting married, so yes, people with autism can live a fulfiling life and a job. If you had told me at 15, I would be working. I would have said yes, and you are going to win the lottery, but in fact, I accomplished the reality of working and supporting people like me. What an achievement for myself this was.

Not everyone is the same that has autism, but if I can do it, you can too. Autism is not caused by:

1. Bad parenting

2. Vaccines

3. Diet

4. An infraction that can spread to people

As I stated before, you are born with autism. Autistic people can have any level of intelligence. Some autistic people have average or above average Intelligence. For example, Albert Einstein was autistic, and he was known for his services to theoretical physics. His intellectual achievements originally resulted in Einstein becoming a genius.

Autistic people may have other conditions:

1. Attention deficit hyperactivity disorder (ADHD) or dyslexia

2. Anxiety or depression

3. Epilepsy

Autism is not visible, it is a disability you can't see, and that is what people forget. The most hurtful thing you could say is he/she doesn't look autistic. No one can define what autism should look like, and these words should not be said.

Autism affects each person differently, and symptoms can change over time. It is not specific to one race or ethnicity. Autism is seen more in boys than girls, there is still so much to learn, and I personally believe first-hand experience is at best.

Autism isn't a weakness personally, I believe it is an advantage, and it is a lifelong journey, and I am here to share this with you.

Diagnosis

To get someone diagnosed, you will need to speak to your GP(doctor), a health visitor for young children under 5, or any other professional you or your child see, such as a doctor or therapist. And Special educational needs Senco staff At your school.

When trying for a diagnosis, write a list of the signs of autism you think you or your child have and bring it with you. Ask people who know you or your child well, like family, teachers, and friends, if they have noticed any possible signs you could add to your list. And try not to talk about other things as the autism diagnosis is what is needed to speak about that rather than irrelevant things.

How Can A Diagnosis Help? Adults And Children

A diagnosis can help you understand your child's needs and how you can help your child or yourself.

As a Parent

Get support from your child's school, and understand your child is not just being naughty and difficult.

Before I was diagnosed, I was known as a difficult and naughty child, the signs of autism I had which led me to be diagnosed were anxiety, emotions, anger, lack of communication, and taking things literally, for example, just before I was diagnosed I was walking around, and the teacher had told me "*Dylan put your bum on that chair*" so I walked over got the chair put it on the back of my bum, and I carried on walking. Because I did what I was told to do, again, this is seen as difficult, but all I did was follow the instructions given.

My anxiety would rise when I was in a classroom with around 30 students making all types of different noises, so I would start to do things in class that would get me into trouble to leave the classroom

Because I couldn't communicate my needs to the teacher. If your child is showing behaviours or frustration, it sometimes may be to not being able to tell you what is actually making your child anxious or upset.

As an Adult

1. Understand why you might find some things harder than other people.

2. Explain to others why you see and feel the world in a different way.

3. Get support at college, university, or at work.

Waiting Time at Autism Assessment

It is not always easy to get an autism assessment. It took my family 2 years to help me get diagnosed.

Waiting times can be very long.

If you're finding it hard to get an assessment, you could speak to someone else and get a second opinion. It may also help to speak to other people like myself who have been in a similar situation.

After I was diagnosed, I struggled personally because I was afraid of being labeled. For example,

Dylan is autistic, or *he is special.* Questions like *do you have autism?* It was the most frustrating thing ever as I am a genuinely happy person, but all people could see was he has got autism, but no one could ever see how hard I tried to be normal, how hard I tried to be like them until one day I realised yes I am autistic, and I was determined to live side by side with my autism and overcome everything I struggle with every day I didn't like crowded places, but I tried every day going to the dining halls surrounded with people, and loud noises. I pushed myself to start taking the bus and socializing. It was tough and hard, and all that determination to be able to do "normal things" made me realise that I could live with autism and make the world a better place and teach people we are not different from anyone else. If anything, sometimes our minds are better. Sometimes I think, hold on, I am a normal person. If I was to arrange to go for a meal at 6:30, I would be there at 6:20, but 8 times out of ten, the neurological person cancels the plans and changes everything. They are the people the don't give specific instructions. No one is a mind reader, but in this world, with all our brains, everyone is different, so you can't just label people who have been diagnosed.

It's Raining Cats and Dogs

Throughout the majority of my life, one of the main struggles was idioms (literal phrases). People often thought I was rude and cheeky. In fact, I just saw exactly what the neurological person was saying

For example, at the age of 16, a teacher approached me and stated, "*Dylan, have you ever caught a bus*" I replied, "*no sir, my arms are not big enough*" I was sent to the head teachers office for being cheeky I can assure you all, I honestly believed you had asked me if I had caught a bus with my own hands, but my teacher never understood my thought process. Now I am 21 years old, and I understand what the teacher meant. He was trying to say, Dylan, have you ever gone on a bus to get to a destination?

Throughout this chapter, you will find idioms that people with autism may take and how a neurological person could approach the answer for a better understanding of each other.

Dylan, you have just hit the nail right on the head.

I took this as if I had a hammer in my hand and smacked a hammer on the nail, which led myself to be distressed because I was telling the teacher I didn't have a nail or a hammer and because I was arguing the fact the teacher was telling lies, but really she was only trying to tell me I had done a great job of answering her question. Today, I laugh at this. Now I understand what it means.

Because I was new to this phrase, I had no knowledge of what it meant. The only knowledge I had was how you hear it, so when I understood what this meant, the next time I had answered the question correctly, she would reply with "*Welldone, Dylan*" because that way, we both understood exactly what was said.

A blessing in disguise.

Someone with autism may not understand this, but what this means is I'm really glad I missed that train turned out to be a blessing in disguise because I saw my best friend for the first time in 6 months, as it is something that appears bad at first but ends up having a good impact

Adding fuel to the fire.

Adding fuel to the fire with this being said to me once before, I didn't understand what this exactly meant. I was in a situation where I had been making things worse, so someone said to me, "*Dylan, Stop adding fuel to the fire*" I replied, "*what are you on about? I don't have any petrol, and they is no fire*" because that's how my mind had heard it and saw it. But a neurological person will understand this as stop making the situation worse," but now someone will say the real meaning behind it.

Idioms can be very hard for people like me to understand, and these idioms can be taught to people like me so everyone can understand how people take them.

For me personally, sometimes, I have done my own research on idioms to help myself understand what they mean. If your child or yourself has some spare time, take 5-10 minutes to learn idioms and the real meaning behind them, this can save future outbursts or anxiety around the meanings.

When I was in school, I was doing an exam for maths. The exam paper asked me to draw a table, so I spent about 10 minutes drawing a replica of my dining table at home because that was what it had told me to do. I didn't understand the question correctly, but I still believe I was correct because the question did not define exactly what to draw; however, I was in a maths exam and not an art exam. Again, the paper asked me to defend my answer, so I added machine guns to my answer with an army and a trench because It wasn't specific, and that is how I understood it.

Communication

You can help yourself or your child communicate better, especially if communicating verbally is hard.

Use your child's name, so they know you are speaking to them. For example, "*Dylan, follow me.*"

Keep the language simple and clear, and speak slowly and clearly. Sometimes if your child is nonverbal, try things like showing them simple gestures or pictures to show support for what you are saying or going to do. For example, show a picture of food if it is time to eat.

Allow extra time for you or your child to process information or what has been said. Sometimes it can be best to try not to ask your child lots of questions and give your child time to process the information. Try not to have a conversation when the environment around them is noisy.

Some autistic people have behaviours, such as repetitive behaviour (such as flapping their hands or flicking their fingers and sometimes tapping). For me personally, when I was anxious, I used to rub my hands back and forth on the top of my legs over and over. I never actually noticed I did this until my family members picked up on it, and whenever I would do this, they would know I was anxious, and they would try and de-escalate the issue. When your child is feeling anxious, try not to give eye contact when communicating, as this could make the situation more overwhelming, and a meltdown could happen.

People with autism may have difficulty developing

language skills and understanding what others say to them.

They also often have difficulty communicating non-verbally, such as:

1. Hand gestures

2. Eye contact

3. Facial expressions

With communication, try not to give specifics as sometimes they can't always be reached. For example, if I was to message my mother and say, "*when will you be home?*" my mom would say 16:10. I have checked the time, and it is now 16:11, and I am getting anxious because she said she would be back a minute before. When giving specific information, try and stick to it as much as possible or barrier this by saying I will be home after I have done this or that, so your child knows what is going to happen and when. Another example is if your child wants to see a relative and you can not give a specific date but know it will be soon, say, "*We can go can see (relative) this month*" rather than "*we will go today or tomorrow.*" This gives enough time for your child to process the information given.

Another example is once before my partner said to me throw me a bag of crisps, so I went and got the packet of crisps, and I threw them at her because that's what she had told me to do. Now I understand all she meant was can you bring me a packet of crisps. This is where there are 2 kinds of specifics. Try and be specific with instructions, and don't be specific with times and dates. Always make sure the communication is clear and simple.

Children with autism are often unable to use gestures such as pointing to an object to give meaning to their speech. They often avoid eye contact, which can make them come across as rude, uninterested, or inattentive. Without meaningful gestures or other nonverbal skills to enhance their oral language skills, many children become frustrated in their attempts to make their feelings, thoughts, and needs known. They may act out their frustrations through verbal outbursts or other inappropriate behaviours.

Myself when I sometimes talk, I may stutter, for example, *Hhhhhhh hello,* this frustrates me very much, and I used to be very embarrassed, but now I take a break, pause, and finish my sentence, or even sometimes my family members finish of the sentence for my as they know the word I am trying to say, also my communication on the phone is also hard to deal with, but I always answer the phone as much as possible to overcome my anxiety.

If your child is showing random and unknown behaviours, it may be your child is trying to explain he needs something, but your child can't physically communicate what is upsetting them. For example, if your child is in pain, he may act out behaviours because they can't tell you they are in pain or maybe that they are hungry, so instead, they act out frustration. For example, I remember once when I was in school. The teacher had asked me where the funniest place was to take a picture. I said it was in "*the bathroom, having a poo*" the teacher pulled me outside and shouted at me for being inappropriate.

That day there was a Friday night school disco, and the head teacher pulled me out of school early and told my parents I could not go, so I showed behaviours because I believed I had done nothing wrong and I was punished. The teacher could have communicated to all the class that it had to be appropriate.

Education

One of the main decisions you will have to make is the type of school you want your child to go to.

You will have to decide this very thoughtfully. For example:

1. **Mainstream school**: mainstream school is a regular school where your child may get support from special educational needs staff if they need it, but mainstream school can't always meet your child's needs. Not everyone in a mainstream school will be diagnosed with something. Mainstream schools will have a large number of people, up to 200 students in each year group.

2. **Special school**: a special school is for children with special educational needs, which could possibly meet the needs of your children to have a successful time in education. Most people in this type of school will maybe have other needs such as ADHD or even sometimes physical needs. Special needs schools will have a reduced amount of students in smaller groups to help prevent students from being overwhelmed.

From my personal experience, as I have been to both a mainstream school and a special school, I can certainly say a special school was more suited for my needs. When I was in mainstream school, I believe I knew I was different from all the other students. I tried to do things other students did because the things I enjoyed doing wasn't really what the other kids did, so I had to change myself socially and physically to be able to fit in such as I enjoyed singing and dancing in my early school days I got on a lot more with girls then I did with boys. Whilst people in my school year were into rap and hip hop, I was into pop, so I had to change myself to fit in and leave the stuff I enjoyed behind. The clothes I wore had to change because otherwise, I couldn't fit into society. It was like having 50 coffees together and 1 single tea. It was noticeable, so I changed it to 51 coffees. This made it a little bit easier for me; however, I wasn't happy being who I was. I enjoyed the music. It helps relieve anxiety. It is the world that makes society hard, and society should relate as everyone is equal no matter what race, gender, or disability. Nothing at all should change how you look at someone.

Moving to a different school that was suited for my needs (special school) made me understand that there are people out there like me. I was accepted for who I was, and I could be myself. Sometimes the teachers didn't always understand, so I helped them understand me, and they also helped me understand the mind of a neurological person

With a few more changes of headteachers, I started to act out on behaviours until one finally stuck and I wasn't longer known as a naughty boy. I finally managed to become a head boy of the whole school and managed to have a fantastic work experience at another school, supporting younger students in an educational setting which I really enjoyed and hoped to work there.

School was a struggle for me, but the only way I was

going to get through school was by managing my autism by challenging my difficulties the best I could, and this is what you hope you can do with your child. Boost them to the highest potential you can.

During a regular college, when I first started, I had an extra support teacher who sat right next to me. I didn't want any of the other students to know why I needed extra help, so I had discreet help. I realised other people would use her as well, and I was then comfortable telling people I was autistic because I was proud of who I was at that time. I did a health and social care course which was full of girls, and I was the only boy in my class. I did health and social care so I could support and look after people with autism in a care setting or within the community, and people were shocked and found that the reason I did health and social care was to help people like me, and they found that really kind and they saw how passionate I was about it even the people in my class pushed me where I was today because I was proud of being who I am, and no one could ever put me down about being autistic.

I am proud to be autistic. This is my life, and I will embrace living with autism. As I completed my first year with a pass, I was in a hurry to get my second year completed and ready to get into work. I didn't know what I was going to do or where to start, but I had a passion before it even started, so I ended up finishing my 2nd year around 4/5 months early, and I was myself all year by challenging my own anxiety of trying to become "normal." I managed this by being social during class, and things like this made it easier during breaks and cigarette breaks. As I smoked, people would speak to me asking for a lighter, so from then, I challenged my anxiety and asked general questions such as how was your day or what course you on every day. These people got easier to speak to, and I was finally able to socialise with pretty much anyone, and this was a big achievement for me.

Sensory needs (Hypersensitivity)

People with autism may have sensitives to:

1. Sights
2. Sounds
3. Touch
4. Taste
5. Smells
6. Balance
7. Awareness of body position and movement
8. Awareness of internal body cues and sensations

Sensory issues may look like this:

1. Increased movement such as jumping, spinning or crashing into things
2. Increasing drumming such as hand flapping, making noises, or rocking back and forth
3. Talking faster and louder or not talking at all
4. Covering eyes or ears
5. Difficulty recognising internal sensations like hunger, pain, or the need to use the bathroom
6. Refusing or insisting on certain foods or

clothing items

7. Frequent chewing on non-food items

8. Frequent touching of others or playing rough

9. Difficulty communicating or responding as the brain shifts resources to deal with sensory input (shutdown)

10. Escalating, overwhelming emotions, or need to escape the situation (meltdown)

You can barrier these types of sensory issues by:

1. Using light cover, sunglasses, or a hat under fluorescent lights

2. Wearing earplugs or headphones in noisy environments

3. Working in spaces with a closed door or high walls

3. Avoiding strongly scented products

4. Choosing foods that avoid aversions to textures, temperatures, or spices

5. Wearing soh comfortable clothing

6. Adjusting schedules to avoid crowds(most shops now have autism-friendly hours), for example, shopping and cinemas

Examples of accommodations for hypersensitivity:

1. Visual support for those who have difficulty speaking information

2. Using fidget toys, chewies, and other sensory tools

3. Arranging furniture to provide safe, open spaces

4. Taking frequent movement breaks throughout the day

5. Eating foods with strong flavours or mixed textures

6. Weighted blankets, lap pads, or clothing that provides deep pressure (sometimes a rucksack with heavy items placed inside may help)

My sensory likes and dislikes have changed all over the years. I remember when I was getting diagnosed, there was a small shaped rectangular box with pins, and if I put my hand into the pins, I could see a hand shape out of pins. I would put my face into it because I liked the feel of the pins. I didn't like the feel of sponges, and sponges made me anxious because of the feel. When I was around 12-13, I could only wear clothes that were cotton. I didn't like the shell suit type of material clothes. I couldn't handle the feeling of it; I still don't know what it is. I just don't like it. I always like pressure around my body like a massage as it relaxes me, and I just feel comfortable with the pressure. I also like sensory lights that move. My Nan once got me a cube that had sensory items around the cube, such as an analogue stick, a moving pinball, a switch, and clicking dots. It was a great thing to have at school. It helped me focus on the teacher talking at the same time and kept my thought process moving.

Special Interests (Obsessions)

Many autistic people, including myself, have intense and highly-focused interests, often from a fairly young age. These can change over time or be lifelong. It can be art, music, gardening, trains, planes, and numbers. For many younger children, it may be Thomas the tank engine, dinosaurs, or particular cartoon characters.

Autistic people might also become attached to objects or parts of objects such as toys, figures, or model cars or more unusual objects like milk bottles, tops, stones, or shoes. An interest in collecting is also known.

A neurotypical person may find this strange. Normally, if you were to lose a family member, you may be very upset. Well, let's think of someone with autism who may have the same care about their special object the same way you would with your family member, so if, for example, (toy) or (stone) was lost or broken, it could set off anxiety and behaviours may show but they may handle it in a different way, and they may take the loss of a relative in a different way as well.

My special interests and objects when I was younger were music, history, and controllers. I had a passion for collecting PS4 controllers, and if I had ever lost a controller or it had been broken, I was very unhappy and upset. From a neurotypical person's point of view, this is seen as replaceable, but these items meant a lot to me and were very special. It caused an emotional meltdown.

Music was a big thing in my life and still is now. I would listen to songs I relate to mainly. I would listen to the same songs over and over on repeat, but that is what I enjoy. My music will rarely ever expand, but that's the structure I liked the same repetitive playlist.

In school, I loved learning history. Pearl harbour was always my favourite to learn about it. I had researched so much about pearl harbour I was correcting my teacher on what happened as she didn't have the information 100%, so I helped her. I wasn't being nasty or rude; I just really wanted to let her know how much I knew about pearl harbour. And it was part of a special interest for me, and I was really pleased with that lesson, and sometimes it was hard for me to engage, but that day I was engaged from start to finish because it involved a special interest. If your child isn't engaging with something, make it fun and get them involved in something they have a passion for, such as if they like trains but don't like the thought of going outside, take them to a countryside train track where the people would be minimum and give it a try as they may be engaged.

Literal Dictionary

Literal idioms from A-Z:

1. A BLESSING IN DISGUISE

Something that appears bad at first but ends up having good results.

Missing that plane turned out to be a blessing in disguise because I got to spend more time with my family.

2. A SANDWICH SHORT OF A PICNIC

A humorous way of saying someone is stupid or is a bit mad.

He brought only shorts and t-shirts when he went to Sweden in the winter – I think he might be a sandwich short of a picnic!

3. A STONE'S THROW

Something is very close to or near.

Luckily the wedding is just a stone's throw from our hotel so we can walk there.

4. ACTIONS SPEAK LOUDER THAN WORDS

What you do is more important than what you say; someone's words may not be trustworthy.

Person A: "John keeps saying he wants to take me out for dinner, but then he never does!"

Person B: "Actions speak louder than words."

5. ADD FUEL TO THE FIRE

When someone does something to make a bad situation worse.

When Sarah started laughing during the argument, it really added fuel to the fire!

6. ADD INSULT TO INJURY

To make a bad situation worse.

As if breaking my arm isn't bad enough, to add insult to injury, I have to pay £1,000 in hospital fees as I didn't have travel insurance!

7. ALL EARS

To be eagerly waiting to hear about something.

Person A: "I have to tell you about what happened on our trip to Spain…"

Person B: "I'm all ears!"

8. AT A CROSSROADS

To be at a point in your life when you need to make an important decision.

I was at a crossroads when I was offered a job in the US, but my boyfriend wanted to stay in London.

9. BARKING UP THE WRONG TREE

To be wrong or misguided about the reason for something

He thinks the company's problems can be solved just by firing the sales team, but he is barking up the wrong tree.

10. BEAT ABOUT THE BUSH

To talk about unimportant things because you are avoiding a particular topic.

Stop beating about the bush! Are you planning to quit university, or not?

11. BETTER LATE THAN NEVER

It is better to do something late than not at all.

Person A: "Sorry I missed your birthday! There's a card in the post." Person B: "Don't worry. Better late than never!"

12. BETWEEN A ROCK AND A HARD PLACE

To be in a difficult situation where both options are bad.

Person A: "If I go to the wedding, mum will be upset, but if I don't go, then I'll be letting down the rest of the family!"

Person B: "Sounds like you're caught between a rock and a hard place."

13. BITE OFF MORE THAN ONE CAN CHEW

To do too much or take something on that is too difficult.

Person A: "I'm going to start that weekend job at the museum on top of my full-time job because I really need the money."

Person B: "Sounds like a lot of work! Don't bite off more than you can chew."

14. BITE THE BULLET

To decide to do something that is difficult or unpleasant but necessary.

You are going to have to bite the bullet and tell your ex (girlfriend) that you need the apartment back.

15. BLOW OFF STEAM

To do something that helps you get rid of stress, energy, or anger.

After my meeting with the boss, I went for a run to blow off steam.

16. BOB'S YOUR UNCLE

To say that a set of instructions or task is simple or easy.

To make the salad dressing, you just put oil, vinegar, honey, and mustard into a bowl, mix them together and bob's your uncle!

17. BOG-STANDARD

Something that is very ordinary or basic, nothing special.

Despite the excellent reviews, we thought the restaurant was just bog-standard.

When learning idioms in English, you need to watch

out for old-fashioned expressions. For example, you probably know the idiom 'It's raining cats and dogs'. However, most Brits would never use this expression now. It is outdated. Instead, we say: 'It's bucketing it down! ' 'It's chucking it down! ' or 'It's pi*sing it down!'.

18. BOTCH/BODGE JOB

Work that has been done badly, in a clumsy, lazy way.

The original builders did such a bodge job of our kitchen that we had to get it completely redone.

19. BUDGE UP

An informal way of asking someone to move to make room for you.

Could you budge up a bit so I can sit down?

20. BUILDER'S TEA

Strongly-brewed English breakfast tea with milk.

I'll have a builder's tea, please.

21. BURY ONE'S HEAD IN THE SAND

To refuse to think about or confront serious issues or situations.

Martin just buries his head in the sand when it comes to his financial problems.

22. BUST ONE'S CHOPS

To work very hard on something or to harass

someone.

I was busting my chops all night to get that report finished! Stop busting my chops! I'll mow the lawn later.

Note: In British English slang, the word 'chops' is used to mean 'mouth'. So the idiom above literally means 'punch in the mouth'.

23. BY THE SKIN OF ONE'S TEETH

To narrowly succeed in doing something.

The traffic was terrible, so we only made the plane by the skin of our teeth!

24. CALL A SPADE A SPADE

To state the truth about something, even if it's unpopular or unpleasant

I know he's your brother, but let's call a spade a spade: he's pretty lazy.

25. CALL IT A DAY

To stop working on something.

It is almost 9 pm. I think we should call it a day and finish the report tomorrow.

26. CHEAP AS CHIPS

When something is inexpensive or good value for money.

It doesn't look like it, but our new sofa was (as) cheap as chips!

27. CHINESE WHISPERS

Information or rumours that have been passed on by many people and are no longer reliable.

John and Maggie from the office haven't actually announced they're getting a divorce. It's probably just Chinese whispers.

28. CHIP ON ONE'S SHOULDER

To hold a grudge/be angry about something that happened in the past, or to be arrogant and think too highly of oneself.

Whenever we mention his childhood, he gets really angry. He's got a chip on his shoulder about it.

The new sales guy at the office has a real chip on his shoulder. He's not even that good!

29. CLAM UP

To become silent or stop talking.

When Bill came into the room, Jenny just seemed to clam up. I think she likes him!

30. COLD FEET

To get nervous or to have second thoughts about doing something

He was getting cold feet about the wedding, but I told him that was perfectly normal.

31. (THE) COLD SHOULDER

To deliberately ignore someone.

I got the cold shoulder from Anna at the party. I guess she's still annoyed with me.

32. COST A BOMB

When something is very expensive.

That Italian meal cost a bomb! We won't be going back there unless we win the lottery!

33. COST AN ARM AND A LEG

When something is very expensive.

The new bar in town was really fancy, but my drink cost an arm and a leg!

34. COUCH POTATO

A lazy person who doesn't do much exercise and spends a lot of time on the sofa watching television.

My husband has turned into a couch potato since he lost his job.

35. COULDN'T CARE LESS

To show indifference to something or a total lack of interest.

I couldn't care less if Harry comes out tonight or not! I don't really like the guy.

36. CURIOSITY KILLED THE CAT

A warning that being inquisitive or curious can get you into trouble.

Person A: "Where are you going at this time of

night?"

Person B: "Curiosity killed the cat!"

37. CUT A LONG STORY SHORT

To get to the point, to not include unnecessary detail.

To cut a long story short, she has to move back to the US until her new visa comes through.

38. CUT CORNERS

To do something in the easiest way possible (usually not very well) in order to save time or money

We had to cut corners to get the project done within our budget and by January.

39. CUT SOMEONE SOME SLACK

To avoid being critical or judgmental of someone (even if they deserve it).

Person A: "Hannah's late for the second time this week!"

Person B: "Cut her some slack! The traffic's awful this morning."

40. CUT TO THE CHASE

To get directly to the point when speaking, to not give unnecessary detail

I have to leave in a minute, so can you cut to the chase? What exactly do you want me to do?

41. DIG ONE'S HEELS IN

To refuse to do something or change your mind, especially when people are trying to persuade you.

I wanted to go on the earlier train, but Mary dug her heels in, so we had to get the later one.

42. DOG EAT DOG (ALSO 'CUT THROAT')

A situation that is very competitive, where people are willing to harm each other's interests to get ahead

The music industry is a dog eat dog these days.

I'd stay out of the legal sector. It can be a cut-throat business.

43. DON'T GIVE UP THE DAY JOB

Used in a humorous way to tell someone they're not very good at something.

Person A: "What do you think of the haircut I gave Hannah?"

Person B: "Don't give up the day job, mate!"

44. DON'T PUT ALL YOUR EGGS IN ONE BASKET

A warning not to put all your resources or efforts into just one thing.

Although you've made an offer on this house, I would still visit some others. You don't want to put all your eggs in one basket.

45. DON'T RUN BEFORE YOU CAN WALK

A warning not to try something difficult before you

understand the basics.

If you're not very good at swimming, I'd stay in the shallow end and keep close to the side. You don't want to run before you can walk.

46. DESPERATE TIMES CALL FOR DESPERATE MEASURES

In a very challenging situation, you need to take extreme action.

She moved to Australia after she found out about her husband's affair. I suppose desperate times call for desperate measures!

47. EASY DOES IT

To slow down or do something slowly/carefully.

Easy does it! Those boxes you're holding are very fragile.

48. EAT A HORSE

To be extremely hungry.

I am so hungry I could eat a horse.

49. (The) ELEPHANT IN THE ROOM

An important and obvious topic that everyone knows needs to be discussed, but that isn't brought up or mentioned.

David leaving the company was the elephant in the room during that meeting. No one wanted to bring it up!

50. EVERY CLOUD HAS A SILVER LINING (often just: EVERY CLOUD...)

Even a bad situation may have a positive aspect to it.

I might have lost my job, but at least I don't have that awful journey into work every day. Every cloud...!

51. FACE THE MUSIC

To accept responsibility for something bad you have done.

I'm meeting Hannah tonight, and it is the first time I'll see her since our argument. I guess I'll finally have to face the music.

52. FIND ONE'S FEET

To adjust or settle into a new environment or situation.

I've only been at the new company for a month, so I am still finding my feet.

53. FINGER IN EVERY PIE

To be involved or have influence in many things (often has a negative association).

Person A: "Steve offered to sell me some secondhand TVs and a holiday to Spain!"

Person B: "That guy's got a finger in every pie!"

54. (A) FISH OUT OF WATER

When someone is (or feels) out of place in a situation.

Judy was like a fish out of water at the kids' party. I don't think she likes children at all!

55. FIT AS A FIDDLE

To be in good physical health.

He's in his 90s, but he's fit as a fiddle!

56. FOLLOW IN SOMEONE'S FOOTSTEPS

To do the same as someone else did before you (often a family member).

All the men in my family are doctors, so I'll probably follow in their footsteps and go into medicine too.

57. FREAK OUT

To become very angry, scared, or excited (can be negative or positive).

I freaked out when I saw The Rolling Stones perform. I'd wanted to see them my whole life!

That Goth at the club freaked me out a bit because he was dressed like a vampire!

58. FULL OF BEANS

Someone who is energetic, lively, or enthusiastic

You're full of beans this evening! You must have had a good day at work.

59. GET OFF ONE'S BACK

When someone won't stops criticising, bothering, or telling you what to do.

I wish she would get off my back about the meeting! I know I have to send the agenda out, but I'll do it in my own time.

60.   GET OUT OF HAND

To become difficult to control.

The protest got out of hand, and the police had to intervene when some demonstrators broke down a fence.

61.   GET OVER SOMETHING

To overcome or move on from a difficult situation.

Moving out of the city for a while might help you get over Harry. (This could be the breakup of a personal relationship/marriage or the person's death)

62.   GET SOMETHING OUT OF ONE'S SYSTEM

Do something you have wanted to do so that you can then move on from it.

I don't drink much anymore; I got it out of my system when I was at university!

63.   GET UP/OUT ON THE WRONG SIDE OF THE BED

To wake up in a grumpy or bad mood for no obvious reason.

You're very argumentative today! Did you get up on the wrong side of the bed or something?

64. GET ONE'S ACT/SH*T TOGETHER

To take action in order to be more effective.

I haven't got any work done this morning – I really need to get my act together!

65. GIVE SOMEONE THE BENEFIT OF THE DOUBT

To believe or trust what someone tells you (even though it might not be true).

Hannah said she missed the exam because her car broke down. I am not sure that was the case, but let's give her the benefit of the doubt.

66. GLAD TO SEE THE BACK OF

To be happy that you no longer have to deal with someone.

I was very glad to see the back of John because he made the atmosphere in the office so uncomfortable.

67. GO BACK TO THE DRAWING BOARD

Start planning something again because earlier attempts were unsuccessful.

The client didn't like our original concept, so let's go back to the drawing board!

68. GO COLD TURKEY

To suddenly and completely stop using an addictive substance.

I gave up smoking by going cold turkey; it was

difficult, but it was also the only thing that worked for me.

69. GO DOWN THAT ROAD

To take a particular course of action, both literally and figuratively.

Let's not go down that road again! It always leads to an argument.

70. GO THE EXTRA MILE

To make more effort than is expected or necessary

Frank is a great asset to our team as he always goes the extra mile.

71. (The) GRASS IS ALWAYS GREENER (ON THE OTHER SIDE)

To mean a person is never satisfied with their own situation. They always think others have it better.

I always think the countryside looks nicer than the city, but I guess the grass is always greener…!

72. GREEN FINGERS

To be good at gardening, able to make plants grow.

I've heard you have green fingers – we'll have to get your advice about our garden!

73. HANG IN THERE

To persist with something, to not give up

Hang in there! I know it is tough but you're almost

halfway through the course.

74. HAVE EYES IN THE BACK OF ONE'S HEAD

To be able to see or sense what's going on all around you, when you can't physically see everything.

You need eyes in the back of your head when you have two small children!

75. HEAD OVER HEELS (IN LOVE)

To be extremely in love with someone.

They're head over heels in love with each other!

76. HEARD IT ON THE GRAPEVINE

To hear news about something from someone else, not directly

I heard (it) on the grapevine that you and Alex are splitting up. Is that true?

77. HIT THE BOOKS

To start studying seriously.

After dinner, I'm really going to hit the books. Not much time left before my exams!

78. HIT THE NAIL ON THE HEAD

To be completely right or correct about something.

I think Lucy hit the nail on the head when she said there's no such thing as an ideal school. There are pros and cons to all of them.

79. HIT THE ROAD

To leave somewhere or start a journey

It's getting late, so I'm going to hit the road.

80. HIT THE SACK

To go to bed in order to sleep

It's been a long day, so I'm going to hit the sack. Night night!

81. HOLD YOUR HORSES

Another way of saying 'Wait a moment' or 'don't rush'.

Person A: 'The train's at 9. Grab the bags, find your shoes and call a taxi! ' Person B: 'Hold your horses! We've got plenty of time. '

In English, there are many ways to say 'Wait a moment'. Next time you want to express this idea, try one of the following expressions: 'Wait a sec' (second), 'Hang on a tick' (like of a clock), 'Give us a mo' (moment).

82. IGNORANCE IS BLISS

Sometimes it's better not to know all the facts about something.

Person A: "Did you know that cake you just ate was 600 calories?"

Person B: "I didn't…ignorance is bliss!"

83. IT'S NOT ROCKET SCIENCE

To say something isn't very complicated.

You just need to fill in the form, and you'll get an e-ticket. It's not rocket science!

84. JUMP ON THE BANDWAGON

To join an activity, trend, or opinion that has become popular.

Everyone thinks Boris is going to win the election, so they've jumped on the bandwagon.

85. JUMP SHIP

To leave or abandon a difficult situation.

I don't think the company is going to survive. We should probably jump ship!

86. KEEP ONE'S CHIN UP

To encourage someone to stay positive in a difficult situation.

It's been a difficult month for you but keep your chin up! It will get easier.

87. KILL TWO BIRDS WITH ONE STONE

To achieve two things at once.

I could pick up the dry cleaning on my way to the doctor. That way, we'd be killing two birds with one stone.

88. LEAVE NO STONE UNTURNED

To do everything you can to achieve something.

During the firm's financial audit, they left no stone unturned.

89. LET SLEEPING DOGS LIE (often just: LET IT LIE)

To leave a situation as it is in order to not make it worse.

Don't bring up what happened at Alison's party again. You should just let it lie.

90. LET SOMEONE OFF THE HOOK

To avoid being punished for something or to avoid doing something.

It was my turn to do the washing-up, but mum let me off the hook because I wasn't feeling well.

91. LET THE CAT OUT OF THE BAG

To reveal a secret by accident.

Their engagement was meant to be a secret, but Adam let the cat out of the bag!

92. LOOK LIKE A MILLION DOLLARS

To look very good, often due to what you're wearing.

You look like a million dollars in that black dress!

93. LOSE ONE'S TOUCH

No longer able to do something as well as you could before

I tried to chat a girl up at the bar the other night, but

47

she just ignored me. I must be losing my touch!

94. MISS THE BOAT

To be slow and not take an opportunity when it's offered to you.

I would call the company back now about the job and not wait until the morning. You don't want to miss the boat!

95. NIP (SOMETHING) IN THE BUD

To stop something at an early stage, before it has a chance to develop.

I've noticed that people are starting to arrive late for work. I think we need to have a meeting about it and nip this in the bud before it becomes a real problem.

96. NO PAIN, NO GAIN

You need to suffer or work hard to get what you want or deserve.

Person A: "That gym class was so hard I thought I was going to pass out!" Person B: "No pain, no gain!"

97. NO-BRAINER

An easy decision, something you don't need to think too hard about.

Person A: "Do you think I should get travel insurance before I go to Nigeria?" Person B: "That's a no-brainer. Of course, you should!"

98. NOT ONE'S CUP OF TEA

Something you don't like or are not interested in.

She's a great cook, but the meal she made really wasn't my cup of tea. It was far too spicy.

99. OFF ONE'S TROLLEY/ROCKER/NUT/HEAD

Someone who acts very strangely, seems crazy or insane.

You must be off your trolley if you think I'm going to climb up there! It's way too high!

100. OFF THE TOP OF ONE'S HEAD

From memory, without a lot of thought or consideration

Off the top of my head, I think we're expecting about 18 guests for the party, but I'll check to make sure.

101. ON THE BALL

To be alert and quick to understand and react to things.

You really need to be on the ball in this job because it's fast-paced with lots happening all the time.

102. ON THE PULL

To go out with the intention of finding someone to have sex with.

Those lads on the dance floor look like they're on the pull tonight!

103. ON THE STRAIGHT AND NARROW

To live in a way that is honest and moral, to stay out of trouble.

He was very wild for many years, but he seems to have grown up, and he's on the straight and narrow now.

104. ONCE IN A BLUE MOON

Something that happens rarely.

I eat McDonalds once in a blue moon when I feel like a treat!

105. PIECE OF CAKE

Something that is very easy.

My English exam was a piece of cake.

106. (AND) PIGS MIGHT FLY

Something that will never happen or is very unlikely.

Person A: "I'm going to play tennis at Wimbledon one day!" Person B: "And pigs might fly!"

107. PITCH IN

To join in, contribute or help with something.

If we all pitch in, we can get Charlie a really nice birthday present.

108. PLAY IT BY EAR

To plan something in an improvised way (instead of planning ahead), deciding what to do as the plan develops.

Person A: "Shall we have dinner before or after the cinema on Friday?"

Person B: "Perhaps we should just play it by ear – we don't know how hungry we'll be."

109. PULL SOMEONE'S LEG

Tease or joke with someone by saying something that's not true

You're pulling my leg! I don't believe you met Elton John at the pub!

110. PULL ONESELF TOGETHER

To regain control of your emotions after you've been upset, to calm down.

You need to pull yourself together! Stop worrying about work so much.

111. RAISE ONE'S GAME

To make an effort to improve at something or perform better

You'll need to raise your game if you're planning on beating Anna's time in the half marathon.

112. RING A BELL

When something seems familiar, or you've heard it before.

Person A: "Do you know Hannah Stewart?"

Person B: "That name does ring a bell, but I can't think why."

113. ROCK THE BOAT

To do or say something that could cause a problem or disturbance

The kids are all getting along fine at the moment, so let's not rock the boat.

114. RULE OF THUMB

Judging a situation by experience rather than an exact assessment

As a rule of thumb, you should use two cups of water for one cup of rice.

115. SCRATCH SOMEONE'S BACK

To do someone a favour in the hope that it will be returned can relate to corruption (commonly used as: You scratch my back, I'll scratch yours)

My boss got caught taking free holidays from a company client! I think it was a case of "you scratch my back, I'll scratch yours".

116. SEE EYE TO EYE

To agree with someone

We don't see eye to eye when it comes to politics, but I do like her as a person.

117. SHED LIGHT ON (SOMETHING)

To reveal information about something or to clarify something.

You were in the office on Tuesday when the incident

took place, so perhaps you could shed some light on it for us.

118. SHOOT FROM THE HIP

To speak honestly and directly or to react to a situation very quickly without thinking it through

Person A: "What do you think we should do about Harry's poor sales this quarter?"

Person B: "If I can shoot from the hip, I'd say he probably needs to leave."

119. SIT ON THE FENCE

To adopt a position of compromise, take neither stance on an issue, not yes or no.

There are a lot of people still sitting on the fence over Brexit.

120. SIT TIGHT

To wait patiently

Sit tight! The nurse will be with you in just a moment.

121. SLEEP ON IT

To delay making a decision for a short period of time

You don't have to decide straight away. Why don't you sleep on it and let us know in the morning?

122. SMELL A RAT

To suspect someone is a traitor, behaving illegally, or is up to no good

I thought I could smell a rat when john refused to give me a straight answer about his sales figures! Now we know he's been stealing from the company.

123. SO FAR, SO GOOD

To express satisfaction with how a situation is progressing.

Person A: "How is the building work going?"

Person B: "So far, so good…the house is still standing!"

124. (A) SPANNER IN THE WORKS

Something that prevents or disrupts an event from happening.

We had invited everyone round for a BBQ today, but the rain has really thrown a spanner in the works!

125. SPEAK OF THE DEVIL

Said when the person you are talking about appears unexpectedly

Did you hear about what happened to Michael? …Oh, speak of the devil, here he is!

126. SPILL THE BEANS

To reveal information that was secret.

We are throwing David a surprise birthday party, but please don't spill the beans!

127. SPLASH OUT

To spend a lot of money on something.

We splashed out on new phones for the whole family.

128. STAB SOMEONE IN THE BACK

To betray or hurt someone who trusts you/

This industry is so competitive; it's easy to get stabbed in the back by your closest colleagues.

129. STEAL SOMEONE'S THUNDER

To take attention or praise away from someone else's accomplishments by outdoing them with your own.

My sister is always stealing my thunder – I announce I'm getting married, and she tells everyone she's pregnant!

130. STICK TO ONE'S GUNS

To refuse to change your mind or beliefs about something.

I really respect Sarah. She always sticks to her guns, even if others disagree.

131. STRAIGHT FROM THE HORSE'S MOUTH

Information straight from the person who saw, heard, or experienced the event.

Person A: "Are you sure Andy is quitting his job?"

Person B: "Positive. I heard it straight from the horse's mouth!"

132. TAKE THE MICKEY (or TAKE THE PI*S)

To make fun of someone, or to take liberties.

Dave's a laugh, but he always takes the mickey out of you down the pub.

£4 for a cup of coffee? They must be taking the pi*s!

133. TAKE (SOMETHING) WITH A PINCH OF SALT

To doubt the accuracy of what someone is telling you

I would take Sam's motoring advice with a pinch of salt. He doesn't actually know much about cars.

134. (A) TASTE OF ONE'S OWN MEDICINE

When someone does something unpleasant, and the same is wished on him/her

My boss is a real bully. Someone should give her a taste of her own medicine!

135. THE BALL IS IN YOUR COURT

It is up to you to take the initiative or make the next move.

I've told you how I feel about the wedding, so the ball's in your court now.

136. THE BEST OF BOTH WORLDS

Where you can enjoy the advantages of two different things at the same time– an ideal situation.

He lives in England during the summer and lives in

Australia during the winter months, so he gets the best of both worlds.

137. THE LAST/FINAL STRAW

The last in a series of bad things to happen, when your patience has run out

When the dog destroyed their antique furniture, it really was the final straw. After that, they decided to give poor Rex away.

138. THROUGH THICK AND THIN

To continue to support someone even during difficult times.

John and Chloe have stayed together through thick and thin.

139. TIME FLIES WHEN YOU'RE HAVING FUN

When you're enjoying something, time seems to move faster, and you don't notice the passing of time

I can't believe it's 10 pm already! Time flies when you're having fun!

140. TWIST SOMEONE'S ARM

To convince someone to do what you want them to

I didn't want to go out tonight, but Ruth twisted my arm!

141. UNDER THE WEATHER

Not feeling very well, a little sick

Sarah's not going to come out tonight. She's had a busy week and is feeling under the weather.

142. UP IN THE AIR

A decision or plan is uncertain or unsure.

Person A: "Are they still getting married?"

Person B: "We don't know, as it's all up in the air at the moment."

143. WASTE NOT, WANT NOT

If you use what you have to the full, then you won't desire or need more.

Person A: "Are you going to finish those carrots on your plate?"

Person B: "If not, I'll have them. Waste not, want not!"

144. WE'LL CROSS THAT BRIDGE WHEN WE COME TO IT

To deal with something when it happens rather than worrying about it before.

Person A: "What if there's bad traffic on the motorway?"

Person B: "We'll cross that bridge when we come to it ".

145. WILD GOOSE CHASE

A hopeless pursuit, something that is unattainable.

We were told that if we searched the library archives, we might get some answers, but it turned out to be a wild goose chase.

146. WOULDN'T BE CAUGHT DEAD

Dislike or would never do something.

I wouldn't be caught dead wearing those shoes – they're so ugly!

147. WRAP ONE'S HEAD AROUND SOMETHING

To understand something that is complicated or shocking.

I can't wrap my head around why Megan would leave London for Rotherham!

148. YOU CAN SAY THAT AGAIN

To agree with someone.

Person A: "It's absolutely boiling in here!" Person B: "You can say that again!"

149. YOU CAN'T JUDGE A BOOK BY ITS COVER

Warning not to judge someone or something just based on appearance.

Person A: "I've only met Richard a couple of times, but he seems a bit shy."

Person B: "You can't always judge a book by its cover. He's actually a really outgoing guy once you get to know him!"

150. YOUR GUESS IS AS GOOD AS MINE

To have no idea about something.

Person A: "Do you think Ivan is going to remember all 150 idioms in this guide?!"

Person B: "Your guess is as good as mine!"

151. ZOOM AWAY, ZOOM OFF

Meaning: to be in a hurry.

Example: The duo just zoomed off in the mist, the perfect ending to a fairy tale wedding. Read on

152. ZERO TOLERANCE

Meaning: the denial to allow rebellious activities, usually by rigid and strict application of the rules;

Example: There is zero tolerance towards any gender bias in this company.

153. ZIP YOUR LIP

Meaning: to stop talking.

Example: Why don't you just zip your lip? I am tired of being nagged all morning.

My Story

This is the most important part for me to talk about. This is my story about living with autism in day-to-day life. I started off with a hard setup as a teenager, but towards the end, you will see me become the person I am now with all the things that have affected me.

Education: School

Things started to appear when I was in year 3. I had 3 teachers in one academic year who happened to make me act out behaviours during school as I didn't like change. I would get used to one teacher, and the teacher ended up changing the reason why I was showing behaviours was due to the fact of CHANGE. Most likely, someone with autism does not react to change very well, and in this situation, I didn't react well. I was known for being naughty due to the fact I had not been diagnosed yet. I was diagnosed from the age of 12, and moving to secondary school, teachers and my parents started to pick up on signs of autism.

For example, when I was in class, a teacher had said to me, "*pull your socks up, Dylan,*" so I reached down to my socks and pulled them up. Of course, this is not what he meant. The teacher was trying to tell me I could do better. Because of my autism, I happen to take things literally, and I struggled with this as I used to get into trouble for seeing it how it was heard and not the real meaning behind it. Another example, my parents once told me when I was showing anxiety about not going out that door, so I went out the window and left the house, so we decided to barrier this by saying don't leave the house at any stage.

During the early stages of secondary school, I knew I was different from everyone else. I was labelled as autistic, and the hurtful things that were said were he doesn't look autistic, no one can look autistic it's a disability you can't see as the brain is wired differently, which makes me think differently to someone who is neurotypical now being able to be in a school setting with autism I knew I had to change my appearance to fit in this. I stopped wearing unusual clothes and started to dress like the other children in my school. I wasn't happy doing this, but it got me through some tough times.

I was not good at social activities and mostly did things alone, so I started to play video games with people from school, which then led to easier friendships in person, and things started to get better socially. I enjoyed things like singing and dancing. I opened up a YouTube channel and made a singing video cover of Carly Jepson; *call me maybe.* This resulted in me being severely bullied for a long time, which resulted in me trying to take my own life. I got the help I needed from a specialist after trying to take my life. This meant I could no longer go to a normal mainstream school, so I ended up going to a special school which was not for me as the special school I went to ended up being next to my mainstream school, and I was still getting bullied from people that wasn't even in my school behaviours then started to act out. I started to show aggression outside and inside of school, which led to me not being able to cope with my emotions.

I got on more with girls than I did with boys and was easier to talk to because of the types of music I listened to. It led other students to start thinking I was gay, and this upset me because just because I may act and think in a different way should not label me as being gay.

After around 9 months, I ended up moving to a school that was better suited for my needs, and there were more people like me. This made me feel more comfortable, but the teachers wasn't the best at understanding me, so I tried to help them understand, and nothing was going anywhere. This was when I knew I wanted to help people like me cause I feel I have an understanding of how they think a little bit more than someone neurotypical. I turned myself around with my behaviours and learned to try and become known as "normal" I managed to become the head boy of the school, and I started a work placement at a school I loved so much I wanted to work there, but unfortunately due to travel issues I couldn't participate any longer during my time at school this was when I decided to learn literal meanings a lot, so I had a lot of knowledge in what they mean being in a school like this we all had knowledge each student had some type of needs.

As I mentioned before, too, I was about to finish my final year in school. My teacher had asked me if I had ever caught a bus even though I had read up on idioms and literal meanings. This was something I had not come across. I replied to my teacher no, my arms are not big enough. This led me to being punished, and I left that exact day as I was placed into a school suited for my needs but couldn't accommodate the way I think. This is what made my final push to help people with autism like myself and eventually move on into a school because I can help people like me achieve their potential by being understood and not punished for how their brains may be wired. At this moment, I knew I needed to try my best to think like a neurotypical human being.

During my days in school, I had certain strategies I

used to sit next to my teacher to assist in stopping myself from being distracted in the classroom because I knew If I didn't, I wouldn't focus on the lesson, which also brought my ADHD into place. Sometimes, I couldn't sit still but then sometimes, I would be still and isolated. There was a room called the quiet room, and it was one of the worst things a school could have had. If any behaviour was shown, you would be restrained in the classroom. This is not what my needs were. My needs were communication, not to be restrained. I was never a threat to staff or students; I was more emotional than physical as I struggled to deal with my emotions. So I had to learn myself to deal with these emotions because I hated being inside that quiet room with a staff member towering over you, forcing you into the room like it was a prison; however, physical restraint isn't always the answer. Sometimes, the correct force may be used, but for someone who is not a threat shouldn't be put in a room like this. If anything, this room made my anxiety higher, so I started to deal with my emotions as quickly as I could to barrier the extra anxiety of being in the quiet room.

Communication, I believe, should always be the first process for someone like me because physical activity could make the situation worse, and with myself struggling to understand the literal sentence, I started to use them once I had the knowledge of what this type of sentence means it was sir "you are adding fuel to the fire" all I wanted was communication not to be held by my arms this was when I was trying to block out my Asperger's and try and be a neurotypical to me, this was the best of both worlds. By being able to live with my Asperger's and in a regular environment, I started to use this strategy in school first to allow me to push to my potential. I'm still not at my highest potential, but someone or I will always be there to push myself further.

During my times at mainstream schools, I always found myself being bullied but also trying to fit in because I was trying so hard that it made it harder for me. I started to be myself. I wasn't into the things I once was because I knew what could happen if I showed everything about myself. Rather than showing people everything about me, I showed them what I wanted them to know about me. This made things a lot easier during school and making friends it's about picking your audience. My friend once told me this in school. He wisely said your problem is you pick the wrong audience. He said you tell them one thing, which wasn't the best place to tell them, but you could say something to me, and it would be fine. Ever since that day, I decided to pick an audience of who I could be myself around and who to tell what I wanted them to know. This was like a barrier for me to stop anything from happening as it did in mainstream school, and to this day, I use the same instruction of picking your audience.

Weight Loss and Boxing

Before I left school, I had a boxing coach come in and teach us how to box. After a few sessions, I realised it started to make me feel relaxed and better about myself during school. I never ever took my coat off, and I would stay in my coat all day. It was mainly a comfort coat. I would say I felt better about myself in it and relieved the anxiety of how I might look after about 6-7 weeks. The coach said why do I always have my coat on it was then I asked myself well, why do I actually always have my coat on? I realised I wasn't happy in my body.

So, just before I left school, I joined a boxing club to help me lose weight and learn to defend myself at the same time. It was great it was two for the price of one joining this club meant I had to socialise, so I pushed myself to let my anxiety and frustration out in training and then push myself to start making friends at the club it was fantastic people would say hello to me walking in, and it just felt comfortable for me to be able to say it back. I most definitely say joining the boxing club hiked my confidence after I went around 100 kg to 90kg just from eating healthy than when the boxing and healthy eating kicked in. By the time I started college, I was down to 70kg. I felt great in my own body and comfortable joining college people that I had known from secondary school didn't even recognise me. Not only did the gym help me lose weight, but I also learned to defend myself and stepped into the ring, and it was one of the best experiences in my life in front of a crowded/loud environment. When I was in that ring, my focus had blocked all sound out, and I was just focusing on my opponent.

Education: College

During college, I studied health and social care. The reason I studied this was mainly because during my education in school, I believed that I didn't have the support that should have been given, and I don't want the next generation to feel like I did. They should have somebody to believe in them and push them to their limits during education. You spend 13 years of your life in education which is a big factor in your childhood. So, I started off wanting to support and help people with autism. This meant I was the only boy in the classroom with around 30 girls. This was hard for me, but it meant pushing myself harder to become the person I am today. I was entitled to extra support for my studying, but I didn't want to take this as I thought if I had extra help, my peers would know I am autistic, and I wanted to keep this private after a few more weeks. Everyone thought it was kind that I wanted to work with autistic people, so eventually, I ended up telling them that I wanted to do it so I could help people like me. I told them I was autistic, and they did not care or see me as autistic they saw me for me, and this is when I knew I am proud to be who I am. I am proud to be autistic. This is my life, and I will embrace living with autism. As I completed my first year with a pass, I was in a hurry to get my second year completed and ready to get into work. I didn't know what I was going to do or where to start, but I had a passion before it even started, so I ended up finishing my 2nd year around 4/5 months early, and I was myself all year by challenging my own anxiety's of trying to become "normal".

I managed this by being social during class, and things like this made it easier during breaks and cigarette breaks. As I smoked, people would speak to me asking for a lighter, so from then, I challenged my anxiety and asked general questions such as how was your day or what course you on every day. These people got easier to speak to, and I was finally able to socialise with pretty much anyone, and this was a big achievement for myself. My dad used to take me to college, and there were days I started getting the bus in a crowded and loud environment. Even with it being like this, I still managed to get to my destination safely, and I always said I could easily do this again.

During college, it was a struggle.

Relationships

Personally, this is a big thing for me to talk about. Throughout my life, I know I have been seen vulnerable during relationships. It was always hard for me to be myself around women, but to get past this, I see relationships as lifelong decisions, not just fun. During my teenage years, I didn't have any luck. I was very loving and caring, I would buy gifts, and I didn't realise that was all they wanted. During my teenage years, I was stupid enough to believe they wanted me for me, so this knocked my trust in women. I was 13 with young love. Whilst in my head, I was already married. This was my downfall as I was then easily led on. However, I stopped relationships and decided to actually understand what they are about and what it actually takes to be a boyfriend, and what a girlfriend is.

I properly started relationships at 16. As my years before happened to be useless for me, and I couldn't understand what was wrong with me. As I started to lose weight, I gained confidence, and I would meet girls in my college and eventually gain the confidence to start pursuing my love life. However, due to personal reasons, which will be in the next book, it didn't go as per plan and ended up knocking me back a thousand years. However, once I started work, I once again started pursuing relationships. As I worked in care, it is a sector with the majority of women. As I started to trust and gain friends, I spoke to people outside of work about things I could work on and what I may be doing wrong. The main thing I had to do was stop letting the past get to the future before a conversation had even started, so I started fresh, and rather than trusting people straight away for me, it had to be earned. I definitely wouldn't say I'm the world's best boyfriend. However, I would say I try and give the person the world and keep her as the happiest girl in the world. I had a serious relationship followed from everything I had learnt, and unfortunately, things did not go to plan. I may not have been the best, but I did give it 100%, and as long as I know that, I believe I can't have gone wrong through all ups and downs.

My only advice through relationships is that be yourself and do not change for anyone to embrace. Being autistic, do not hide it because it will only eat you up; however, if you really love something, just let it go. If it comes back, it's yours forever, and if it doesn't, it was never meant to be.

Work

During college, I was put on work experience (placement). I had to complete this to complete my course. In my first year, I went to a children's day nursery. Although this wasn't my choice, I still gave it my best shot at what it would be like to work. The nursery wasn't for me, but I still continued till the end of my 2nd year. At college, I went to a farm that supported people with learning disabilities and autism. This placement was a fantastic learning and helping these people also get ready for work. I was getting really involved, and it felt amazing. Although it was a placement, it didn't feel like work. I was really settled there. This was when I realised I was ready for work. I didn't always agree with work experience, but if I hadn't done that, I didn't see myself working any sooner. So I started to apply for jobs. I applied for some, and didn't get a response.

On my CV, my first sentence was hello, I am Dylan brown, and I have Asperger's (autism) because I am who I am, and no job can change how my brain works. I had an email to arrange an interview for my current role as a support worker. I felt over the moon, but then the anxiety started to kick in regarding interviews, so I revised this role every day until my interview. When I first had my interview, I was nervous, but I knew if I showed it, they might not hire me, so I tried to become as settled as possible I remember the day like it was yesterday. My parents took me there and drove me home when I was in my interview. I was so nervous and overwhelmed. They asked me my name, and I replied, *"can you ask me the question again, please"* because my anxiety was all around answering wrong, and my leg was shaking underneath the table, but as soon as the actual questions started coming, I started to feel relaxed, and the anxiety started to ease around this time. I started to pick up some shifts back at the children's nursery to make some income and get another feel around work. The day I was at the nursery, my parents came to pick me up early. And I got home, and there was a phone call I answered. It was the job I applied for to say I was successful in my interview after a few years of ups and down and badness. This was the best thing I could have achieved at this point. I never thought I would work, but here, I was supporting people like me in a residential setting. I felt on top of the world. In my first couple of weeks, I was quiet at work and tried my hardest to talk to everyone. As weeks went by, I started to come out of my shell and showed my personality during my experience at school. I couldn't be myself, and I was unsettled, but starting this job with the people around me allowed me to be more of the person I am. I would sing around my workplace and even dance for the staff in school. I would have taken the mic out of it, but the staff enjoyed it and accepted who I was.

I always thought work was always about being professional, but a laugh and joke is allowed for everyone. I remember once I was still very serious about my role. But there was a member of staff in imparticular who said that there was a phone call for me, I answered the phone and started talking only to realise the phone was broken, and it was just the string. It was hilarious, and his personality made me become more like him. Having a joke, laughing with everyone, not at them. I started to realise how far jokes could go and how to take them. This made me realise what a joke is and what is not a joke. I was in the best place I could have been. Sooner or later, Covid-19 was around, and masks had to be worn during work. It was really uncomfortable, and I couldn't get used to the material around my face. As it was a law to be used in my workplace, I had no choice but to wear them, and anxiety would come into place at work, so when I was at home, I would get used to the feel of them over and over so it wouldn't be as much as a problem at work. A few weeks later, I had gone through a rough patch at work which led me to live in a hostel, and I couldn't talk to anyone about it. A member of staff called me one day, and I told them where I was, and I wasn't in a good place. I had hidden away from my parents, and I was feeling down and having thoughts that should not have been there, but as an outsider trying to help me, this made me believe not all neurotypicals see you the same. This member of staff believed in me, and I used the belief to push myself further and bounce back twice as hard one day. I said to myself, after all this bumpy road, *I'm still standing, and I'm standing better than I ever did.* I only ever listen to music I can relate to. That was the song for it, so I got back on track and started back at work and supported in my role the best I could, just like how everyone supported me. Although I had gone through this bumpy road, it never affected the way I supported myself in my role. These are the times when you have to challenge yourself to become a stronger individual at work. I started a quest and was unable to communicate, but in this work setting, communication was key, and this pushed me to my potential as I had to use my voice to talk and pass on what had happened during my shifts, and this made things so much easier outside of work. I became a strong person in my workplace, and I needed to push myself to be like this in the real world, and this built my confidence to an extreme level education and work are known as some of the worst things, but If I didn't push myself through them I would not have been the person I am now, and I have become. I wouldn't change who I am for no one. I love living in the best of both worlds. This is me. This is who I am. I can not change who I am, but I can make this better and barrier the things that make me have anxiety.

The Ending

I would like to end this book by saying if, personally, you are autistic, do not let this bother you.

Embrace your autism, and speak about it.

If you or someone you care for/know may be autistic, do not look at them differently.

Everyone in the world is different.

Just because someone has been diagnosed with autism, it does not label him or her. It just shows how clever they are.

At last, I would say that If you have enjoyed this book, you will be excited about part two.

- **Dylan Brown**

These are my parents – the people who made me the man I am today.

Printed in Great Britain
by Amazon